THE
GODDESS SEKHMET

About the Author

A leading pioneer of modern consciousness research, Robert Masters is known as one of the founders of the Human Potentials Movement. Since 1965 he has been the director of research of The Foundation for Mind Research. He has developed the psychophysical method, which concerns neural and sensory re-education, with Margaret Mead as one of his avid students. As a sexologist, he was an associate of Harry Benjamin, M.D., "the Dean of American Sexologists." He counts G.I. Gurdjieff, Wilhelm Reich, F.M. Alexander, Milton Erickson and Moshe Feldenkrais among those who have most influenced him.

Books he has written or co-authored include the classic *The Varieties of Psychedelic Experience* and *Mind Games*. He lectures and leads tours throughout the world.

To Write to the Author

We cannot guarantee that every letter written to the author can be answered, but all will be forwarded. Both the author and the publisher appreciate hearing from readers, learning of your enjoyment and benefit from this book. Llewellyn also publishes a bi-monthly news magazine with news and reviews of practical esoteric studies and articles helpful to the student, and some readers' questions and comments to the author may be answered through this magazine's columns if permission to do so is included in the original letter. The author sometimes participates in seminars and workshops, and dates and places are announced in *The Llewellyn New Times*. To write to the author, or to ask a question, write to:

Robert Masters
c/o THE LLEWELLYN NEW TIMES
P.O. Box 64383-485, St. Paul, MN 55164-0383, U.S.A.

Please enclose a self-addressed, stamped envelope for reply, or $1.00 to cover costs.

Books Written or Co-authored
by Robert Masters (R.E.L. Masters)

The Goddess Sekhmet and The Way of the Five Bodies
Psychophysical Method Exercises (Vols. I–VI)
Listening to the Body
Mind Games
Psychedelic Art
The Varieties of Psychedelic Experience
Sexual Self-Stimulation
Sex-Driven People
Patterns of Incest
Prostitution and Morality
Sex Crimes in History
The Anti-Sex
The Cradle of Erotica
Eros and Evil
Forbidden Sexual Behavior and Morality
The Homosexual Revolution

Forthcoming:
The Masters Technique
Idols, Objects of Power and Objective Works of Art
The Goddess Kapo: Her Magic and Metapsychology
Exploring the Goddess Sekhmet's Worlds

THE
GODDESS SEKHMET

Psychospiritual Exercises of
the Fifth Way

Robert Masters

Foreword by Kenneth Grant

Introduction by Joan Halifax

1991
Llewellyn Publications
St. Paul, Minnesota, 55164–0383, U.S.A.

First Llewellyn Edition
First Printing

First published by Amity House Inc., 1988
Copyright © 1988 by Robert Masters

Credits

p. xiv: painting by Lillian Morgan-Lewis; pp. xxiii,12: paintings by Martyl; p. 4: art by Deborah Koff, graphic rendering by Cathryn Stewart; p. 22: painting by Diana Vandenburg; pp. iv, xii, xviii, xxiv, xxx, 2, 11, 17, 18, 28, 33, 34, 41, 42, 57–67, 213, 214, 229: from the collection of Robert Masters; p. 52: Metropolitan Museum of Art, gift by Henry Walters.

Library of Congress Cataloging-in-Publication Data

Masters, Robert E.L.
  The goddess Sekhmet: psychospiritual exercises of the fifth way / Robert Masters.
      p.   cm.
  Reprint, with new introd. and glossary. Originally published: Amity, N.Y.: Amity House, c1988.
      ISBN 0-87542-495-3 (hard). — ISBN 0-87542-485-6 (pbk.)
    1. Sekhmet (Egyptian deity)—Miscellanea. 2. Magic, Egyptian.
I. Title.
BF1999.M417   1990
299'.31—dc20
                                                                                    90–45836
                                                                                    CIP

Llewellyn Publications
A Division of Llewellyn Worldwide, Ltd.
P.O. Box 64383, St. Paul, MN 55164–0383

ACKNOWLEDGMENTS

During a period of about one quarter century, I have been actively involved in the Work with the Goddess Sekhmet as it has gradually unfolded, and will surely continue to unfold, throughout this particular existence of mine on a planet which is not the only one where I might have served Her. It is also clear now, in retrospect, that the connection to Sekhmet goes back as far in this lifetime as my recollections are able to take me. It is my belief, beyond proof, of course, that Sekhmet has affected me throughout my life.

I believe, as Rameses II believed it of himself, that I was "born out of Sekhmet." That, for an ancient Egyptian, was a quite different statement from the one often routinely made about being "born of" this or that Deity. To be "born out of" in this case asserts a literal fact and reality existing in spiritual dimensions. I would require a spiritual autobiography to make my case—and one day I may write one, detailing adequately (at least for me) just why I hold to such a belief.

I wish first to acknowledge the Goddess who "seized" me for this Work. Sekhmet is loved by me with the whole of my Being. I look forward to hearing this called "mythomania," or worse, by those who have never known so much as one actual waking moment, either physically or mentally, who have never experienced one shred of objective knowledge, and who are spiritually dead for all practical purposes.

Over the last 15 years I have enabled a great many persons to have, in varying degrees, experiences of what they apprehended as the Goddess Sekhmet. The Goddess has taught and healed and protected and otherwise rewarded and punished. Some of the phenomena associated with and arising out of this Work have been discussed with, and often been taken quite seriously by, Egyptologists, archaeologists, anthropologists, parapsychologists, open-minded psychiatrists and psychologists, philosophers, authorities on magic, myth and religion, and persons of many other backgrounds. Many lives have been changed—sometimes drastically transformed—by the contemporary manifestations of Sekhmet. I acknowledge, without including a roster of names, all of those persons just referred to, but especially the ones who have actively and immediately shared with me the more intense and prolonged experiences of the Goddess Sekhmet's worlds.

I might add that I summarized one such collaboration in the book *Psychic Exploration*, published in 1974 and edited by former astronaut Edgar Mitchell, explorer of both outer and inner space—and the sixth man on the moon. That particular shared experience of Sekhmet, as well as others that occurred over the years, was of very great interest to another friend, the late anthropologist Margaret Mead, who developed her own strong affinity for Sekhmet. Among artists, I will particularly mention the painter Diana Vandenberg, another friend, who did a remarkable portrait of Sekhmet, and who has been described as perhaps the finest Dutch artist since Rembrandt. Two other fine paintings—part of a series—by the American artist Martyl are also included and were done in connection with the Brooklyn Museum's ongoing expedition at the Temple of Mut. And appearing for the first time in this edition is a striking Sekhmet painting by Lillian Morgan-Lewis, also an American. These are all persons who have proved themselves able in their differing ways to expand the now knowable dimensions of human reality. I would also like especially to acknowledge Michele Carrier who took many of the photographs and also shared some early explorations—Michele, where are you? Other photographs were taken by Paula Renee and some valuable organizational assistance came from Candace Cave.

Last, but by no means least, I wish to acknowledge my wife, Jean Houston. No human being has been so important for me in this Work as she, and without her this Work would almost certainly, for many reasons, never have been done. On at least one occasion, early in the Work, I made on the magico-spiritual level a mistake that might well have destroyed me. She then saved my life or, if not my life, then my sanity. The spiritually knowledgeable will know that such an assessment is no exaggeration. The details of my act of folly and my rescue will also be reserved for a future autobiography. Jean has supported the Work through the years, accompanying me to the temples in Egypt and to other places where the Work led me. While she has never been directly involved in this Work—her own soul marches to a different Drummer!—it would be quite impossible for me to overstate her supportive contribution to it.

CONTENTS

*Sekhmet, Lady of the Place of the
Beginning of Time,*

*Sekhmet, Whose Essence is Fire,
Tempestuous, Forever,*

*Great One of Magic, Grant me
success in my endeavor!*

*Blessed be the Name of Sekhmet,
Beloved Her Image!*

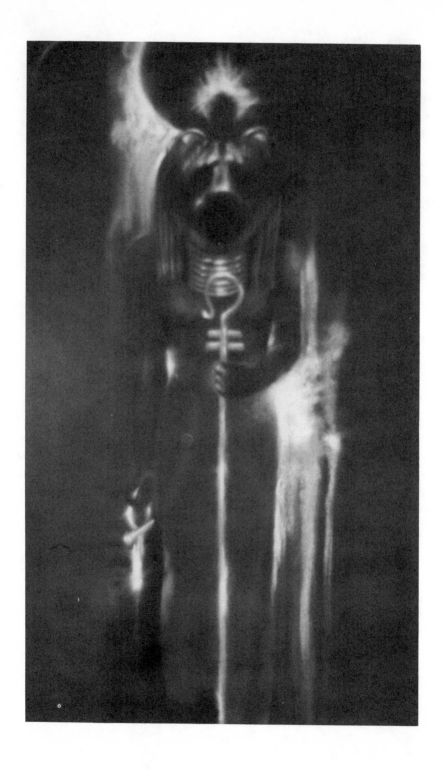

FOREWORD

It does not surprise me that there has been a call for a new edition of this fascinating book. Dr. Masters describes it as a *"scriptural work,"* thus claiming for it a higher than mortal authority—"a means by which a Nonhuman Being...manifests to humans in a way suited to the present consciousness of humans." The reader is warned in no uncertain terms to be prepared "to risk transformation," or to set aside the book. As one who has had experience in these matters, I endorse and underline this warning.

Here are valuable insights and practical formulae for establishing contact with other worlds and lucid descriptions of the magical bodies formulated by the Adept who explores them. The author's unswerving devotion to the Goddess Sekhmet as a Gateway to alien realms is captivating and infectious. Such intensity of aspiration will undoubtedly attract more and more readers, not only those who are fitted for the regimen of exercises provided in the latter part of the book, but those in whom the sense of *devotion* predominates.

Dr. Masters divulges the mystical Mantra of the Goddess, and this, if properly vibrated together with contemplation of the beautiful images of Sekhmet here presented, is sufficient to hurl the soul directly into the presence of the Goddess who grants desires. But it should be remembered that Sekhmet is a goddess of the South, the region of Flame and of the dark god Set, Lord of the Abyss and of the blackening desert sands upheaved by terrible winds that smother all in the Night of Time. One has to tread warily and approach the Goddess with a singleness and purity of purpose such as that which the author himself brings to Her shrine.

Kenneth Grant
London, 1990

INTRODUCTION

Robert Masters is an explorer of not only the contemporary mind but also the mind of history and myth. His extraordinary investigations have taken him through the territories of sex and magic, psychotherapy and psychospiritual practices, psychedelics and symbology. In his book on the Egyptian goddess Sekhmet, he brings into our awareness the presence of Sekhmet as an archetypal force that could well have a profound impact on the human psyche in contemporary Western culture.

Masters indicates that he has been under the sway of Sekhmet for at least three decades. It is clear that Sekhmet has been the ground and fire of his personal initiation. His possession by the goddess has made it possible for him to bring forth her logos, her sacred words as remembered scripture. He has as well introduced the goddess to many who have been taught, healed and chastened by her.

Another fascinating and valuable aspect to his work with Sekhmet is how lost historical, archaeological, mythological and psychological information can be retrieved in non-ordinary states of consciousness. Conventional historical researchers rely on the interpretation of records of stone, wood, clay, bark, cloth and paper. The influence of the Western world view on scholarly works is rarely acknowledged. Masters has obviously done his scholarly homework regarding Egyptian lore; however, his willingness to enter the body of the collective unconscious, and ultimately, the body of the goddess has yielded fascinating results not only for Egyptologists but also for explorers of inner space.

This book is a tribute not only to the goddess Sekhmet but also to Robert Masters' courage, audacity and imagination. The descriptions of his rich psychic experiences in the presence of the goddess are matched by the wealth of psychospiritual exercises that he outlines in the latter part of the book. The description of the "Five Bodies" of the human is a metapsychology that is a metaphysics as well as methodology of transcendence.

Masters has opened the road again for the Egyptian Mystery School to be approached, if not entered. He recalls the main site of worship of the goddess Sekhmet and the gods Ptah and Nefer-Tem at the House of Life in Memphis. It is clear that the goddess Sekhmet is much older than her brother-husband Ptah and her father, the Sun God Ra. She is obviously a form of the Great Mother, one who is the mother of all the gods. Her very name, from the word *sekhem*, which means "strong," "mighty," "violent," implies that the goddess is directly related to the creative and destructive power of the sun. The author sees her strongly associated with Kundalini in the Tantric tradition. Kundalini is the energy of unleashed feminine sexuality manifesting as psychic energy.

Fear of the energy of the goddess, particularly in Western culture, has given rise to a kind of civilizational neurosis. We have almost destroyed our world in our attempts to control the wilderness and wild cultures who inhabit remote regions of mind and earth. Through the psychic archaeology of scholars like Robert Masters, the ancient manifestations of pure energy states are being reawakened so that we can enter the mystery of the untamed. The goddess Sekhmet is an energy key that opens the way to this mystery of an undivided nature.

Joan Halifax
Ojai, California
February 14, 1990

PREFACE AND WORDS OF CAUTION

It is essential, here at the beginning, to state that this volume you now hold may powerfully affect you.

You stand presently at the threshold of a doorway. You are still free to pass through the door or not, as you will decide. Words of caution are offered you to assist you in reaching your decision.

Should you decide you are going to continue, you will inevitably experience the implanting into your brain-mind-spirit of images and ideas emanating from a nonhuman reality the ancient Egyptians called *Sekhmet*. You will become, to at least some degree, a participant in the Goddess Sekhmet's Mysteries, and in the Work of the Fifth Way.

In opening yourself to Sekhmet, you open yourself to direct experience of what for thousands of years have been called the awe-ful and numinous powers of the Divine and the Magical. You may eventually be led to fulfillments greater than any you have yet imagined. You may be seized by Sekhmet, and then unspeakable horrors as well as indescribable delights are among the possibilities. It is always so when one "falls into the hands of the Living God."

Understand, then, that this is a *scriptural* work, a means by which a Nonhuman Being of the Order of Beings known as Gods and Goddesses manifests to humans in a way suited to the present consciousness of humans. Understand that such works penetrate into the whole Being—body and mind and spirit, conscious and unconscious, cells and souls.

Therefore, this book has the power to drastically change you, to alter your reality more or less extremely. If it leads deeply into the Fifth Way, then you will awaken to recognize that you have been living in a kind of demented dream, close to the edges of both madness and death. After that, you will need guidance in a world very strange to you, where wakefulness and sanity threaten to consume you with their radiance. If you are unwilling to risk transformation, then by all means set this book aside now!

But if you decide to continue—the Words of Caution have been provided.

And now, other words—something about how it was that this book came to be. It began—speaking just of the writing of the book—when the scribe-author of much that is communicated here sat entranced before a statue of the Goddess. His eyes open, he first perceived a glowing at the base of the statue. Then, an aura of red flowed around and beautifully illuminated the whole figure. The lioness-headed Goddess, who had been seated, stood and communicated with him, as it seemed to him, telepathically. He did not *hear* the voice, but was told that he would receive information of importance, which he must make every effort to preserve.

He was told that certain sacred books of Sekhmet had been lost, pillaged from the temples and destroyed by unbelievers, while others had been carried off by ignorant people who failed to recognize their value and allowed them to disintegrate. In time, the information contained in many of these books would be disclosed, adapted to the needs and understandings of contemporary humans. Among these books were:

SEKHMET-RA: THE BOOK OF LIGHT

SEKHMET-PTAH: THE BOOK OF IMAGINATION

SEKHMET-BAST-HATHOR: THE BOOK OF GOOD AND EVIL

SEKHMET-ISIS: THE BOOK OF LOVE

SEKHMET-GETESH: THE BOOK OF LUST

SEKHMET-PTAH-THOTH: THE BOOK OF INSPIRED WISDOM

SEKHMET-PTAH-ANUBIS: THE BOOK OF DEATH AND REBIRTH

SEKHMET-HIKE: THE BOOK OF THE KNOWLEDGE OF PAST AND FUTURE

Now, a soft blue light flowed out from the eyes of Sekhmet and the scribe's eyes closed. Before him appeared, standing upright, a beautiful black cat the size of a leopard. It wore around its neck a golden collar studded with red stones glowing from within. With this guide, he passed first into a room where an eternal fire was kept. And this fire was fueled by the skeletons of many kinds of creatures, placed upon the blaze by a procession of tall, slim, graceful black women who were naked except for golden, ruby-studded collars and a diadem engraved with a death's head, serving to indicate their calling. All of these women, he knew, were princesses of tribes of the ancient Libyan Lands, and they could never perish so long as the Breath of Life of Sekhmet was upon them.

He was escorted to an altar by tall, powerful figures wearing breastplates of leather, human-bodied, but with the heads of birds—the predatory beaks and fierce, burning eyes of hawks.

A priestess with red hair, whose beauty astounded him, burst into flames and was consumed. A green snake came and slithered through the ashes. A dwarf came, dragging an ankh larger than himself, paused to read the message on the floor, and then went on. A large bird, wearing a Sekhmet amulet, flew slowly three times in a circle around the hieroglyphics. Then the meaning was revealed: *The Temple of Sekhmet is the Womb of Visions.*

All around him the fleshy walls of the temple were glistening and wet, bathed red by the dancing of the sacred and invisible flames. The walls rippled, sometimes lightly convulsing, the spasms generating phantoms of shadows, these assuming briefly vivid color, depth, life, and then dissolving back into shadowy forms from which new images emerged, taking on the aspect of a surreality.

Images sinuously weaving their way up, from within obscure places in himself, passed out of his body and intermingled with the temple images, interacting with them, assuming the same brief vivid reality, then dissolving as new forms replaced them. He no longer could determine which forms emanated from his body and which appeared to be the children of the temple. His emotions and sensations were experienced in identification with first one visionary being and then another, pale at first, gaining high intensity, diminishing, as the forms first emerged, vivified, and then dissipated in an incessant flowing of becoming, being, slipping away towards nonbeing, to be born again in the becoming of something new and different—human, animal, or combining elements of both.

Surrounded by the undiluted blackness of void, his body,

xxii

which he now observed from a distance, was white as if made from ivory. It gleamed as it drifted, slowly circling, as the weightless bodies of astronauts might drift and slowly circle in space. The body appeared to diminish in size, and he reasoned that this meant an increasing distance between the body and his perception of the body, the means of the perception being a mystery. He decided that he must be dying or had died, and found himself calling four times the name of Sekhmet, hoping that by Her intervention his life might be saved or restored.

Within the temple, the walls were alive and writhing with serpents, intertwining with the long and richly jeweled fingers of women. Seated on Her throne, centered in a circle within which light was seen rising out of symbols, was Sekhmet, unmoving center above the circle, which was spinning.

He felt himself to be in the Presence of the living Sekhmet, from Whom he could not bear to be separated.

Then he no longer knew who he was, or that he was.

He was told later that his body in the chair moved into the exact posture of the Sekhmet statue seated on its throne. And his face became the face of Sekhmet.

There was an apparent infusion of power into his body, as if his body were being charged with some actual physical energy, causing it to become visibly more powerful. Furthermore, he seemed to experience an enrichment of every capacity, his presence becoming mythic, superhuman, for those who were observing him.

Next, there was an abrupt dissipation and deflation, as if too much had been fed in too soon. As if body-mind, menaced, reflexively rejected and expelled the Force that could not be any longer tolerated. Or as if the Force were all at once withdrawn, the danger being recognized by the intelligence directing the infusion.

After that, just before the trance terminated, there was brief contact with what was taken at the time to be a secondary personality, speaking through him with a voice that was very curious, as if the speaker vacillated between being male and female. The words:

I will Teach and you will learn. In many ways I will Teach. In many ways you will learn. The Work will be done.

INVOCATION OF SEKHMET

As it was at Memphis,
So be it now!

Hear me, I beseech Thee,
O Powerful One!

Lady of Rekht,
Lady of Pekhet,
Lady of Set,
Lady of Rehesaui,
Lady of Tchar and of Sehert!

Mother in the Horizon of Heaven,
In the Boat of Millions of Years,
Thou art the Great Defender!
Thou art Overthrower of Qetu!
Preserve us from the evil chamber
of the souls of Hes-hra!
Deliver us from
the Abode of Fiends!

O Thou Who Art

Sekhmet,
Life-Giver to the Gods,

Sekhmet,
Lady of Flame,

Sekhmet,
Great One of Magic,

Sekhmet,
Eternal Is Thy Name!

O, Hear me now!

Sekhmet,
With Lioness head,

Sekhmet,
Whose color is Red,

Sekhmet,
Daughter of Ra,

Sekhmet,
Consort of Ptah,

Sekhmet,
Mighty Is Thy Name!

O, Hear me now!

Sekhmet,
Goddess of Pestilence,

Sekhmet,
Goddess of Wars,

Sekhmet,
Queen of the Wastelands,

Sekhmet,
Terrible Is Thy Name!

O, Come to me!

Sekhmet,
Destroyer of Rebellions,

Sekhmet,
Scorching Eye of Ra,

Sekhmet,
Protector, Ruler,

Sekhmet,
Holy Is Thy Name!

O, Reveal Thyself to me!

Sekhmet,
Mother of the Gods,

Sekhmet,
Mistress of the Crowns,

Sekhmet,
Thou art called Only One,

Sekhmet,
Beloved Is Thy Name!

Possess me now, O Great One!

Sekhmet,
Greater than Isis,

Sekhmet,
Greater than Hathor,

Sekhmet,
Greater than Bast,

Sekhmet,
Greater than Maat,

Sekhmet,
Mysterious Is Thy Name!

I am lost in mystery!

Sekhmet,
Pre-eminent One,

Sekhmet,
Light beyond Darkness,

Sekhmet,
Sovereign of Her Father,

Sekhmet,
Hidden Is Thy Name!

Rapturous my dying!

Lady of Amt,
Lady of Manu,
Lady of Sa,
Lady of Tep-nef,
Lady of Heaven!

Thou art Ammi-seshet,
Destroyer, Upholder!
Thou art the Terror
Before Which fiends tremble!
Thou art Lust!
Thou art Life!
Ever-Burning ONE!

Tekaharesa-Pusaremkakaremet,
Sefi-per-em-Hes-Hra-Hapu-Tchet-f,
Mistress of Enchantments,
Source and Word of Power,
Forbidden Is Thy Name!

I am the sealed one!

Do not consume us
With Thy Fire,
Give us Light!

O Lady, Mightier than the Gods,
Adoration rises unto Thee!
All beings hail Thee!
O Lady,
Mightier than the Gods!

Preserved beyond Death,
That Secret Name,
O Being
Called Sekhmet.

At the Throne of Silence,
even, shall no more
be spoken than
Encircling One!

I lose myself in Thee!

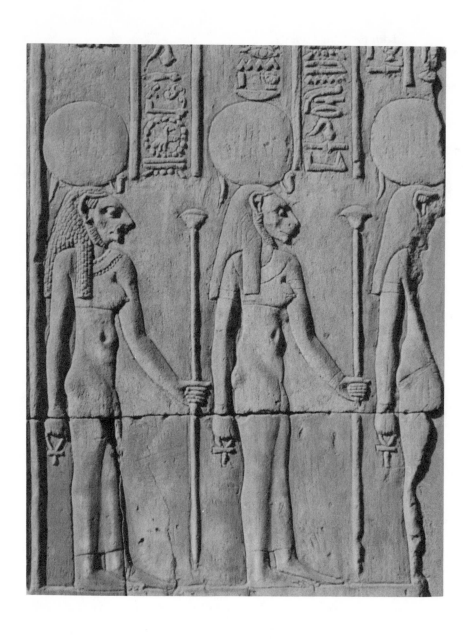

THE GODDESS SEKHMET
FOR THIS BOOK

I am the One Who Knows the Way In and the Way Out.

This Book introduces a Fifth Way—The Way of the Five Bodies, as it was in Egypt, but also New Knowledge blended with the Old—to Open the Fifth Way.

This Book Serves the Purposes of Sekhmet and of Humans.

It fulfills the need to *Multiply the Images of Sekhmet.*

All of Time is to Me nothing more than the Flick of a Cat's Whisker. But *Now* is the Time for *This* Work.

On the Night called Sekhmet, All Humans Will Dream the Same Dream. Then, what do you think they are going to Open their Eyes to?

The Cat Has Been Let Out of the Bag!

HUMANS MUST NOW SUPPORT THE NEW TEMPLE OF SEKHMET: THE FIFTH WAY.

Then, the Greatness that once was will become the Greatness Now—not the same, but as it should be and must be!

Sekhmet *does Bless this Work.*

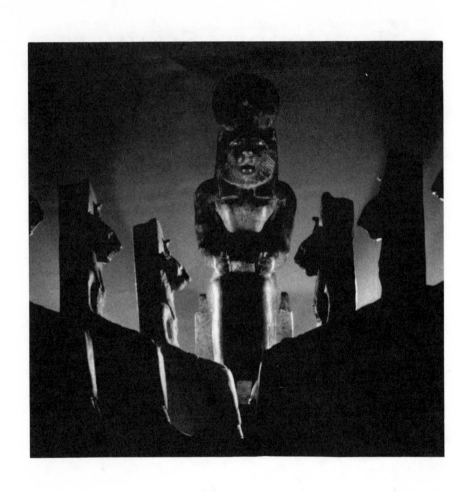

THE WAY OF
THE FIVE BODIES

According to an extremely ancient tradition, distorted variations of which are a part of many religious, spiritual, magical and occult systems, the human being has five bodies, all interactive, but each one having a dimension or reality in which it lives and functions and which is of the same substance as that body. These bodies, and realms, in order of subtlety are the (most subtle) Spiritual Body (Egyptian: SÂHU) and the increasingly less subtle: Magical Body (KHU); Shadow (HAIDIT); Double (KA); and Physical Body (AUFU).

"The Way of the Five Bodies" requires a consciousness which simultaneously differentiates each of the five while, at the same time, all of the five are *functionally* integrated. There is a meta-psychology and a methodology for achieving this ideal and, as well, an underlying metaphysic. The Way is practical and realizable, although extraordinarily demanding. It can explain much and lead to accomplishments which would otherwise be impossible. If it is humanly valid, then it is not just "Egyptian," although its known source is the magico-spiritual Way of the Goddess called *Sekhmet* by the Egyptians. I will discuss the metaphysic briefly, the meta-psychology, which can be tested, in considerably more detail.

According to this Way, there are two primordial, co-existing, interactive and absolutely antagonistic realities: Cosmos (the

3

Powers and Principalities of Order) and Chaos (the Disordered Powers and Principalities). The essentially irrepresentable Powers are functionally represented by *Neters*, or beings experienced by humans as Gods and Goddesses, angels and demons, and others known to religion and mythology. These Powers in their Principalities and for us are hierarchical and, in our terms, good or evil. They are locked in a thus far perpetual struggle, each seeking the other's transformation. They are indestructible, but subject to *transformation* so that a final resolution would be the transforming of Chaos into Cosmos, or that of Cosmos into Chaos. Out of this conflict, sometimes called The War in Heaven, have arisen "intermediate" realities, including the human.

The whole of reality has substance but is neither "material" nor "spiritual," and it is more or less subtle in varying degrees. Much of it is altogether inaccessible to and unknowable by humans. Some of it can be glimpsed or revealed, but not participated in by human beings. Within an exceedingly narrow sector of the whole of reality is the dimension of the human.

The *present situation* may be very roughly described in the following manner, with references to positioning in space understood as a convenience and not essentially veridical. At the "bottom" is Chaos, a realm of such subtlety that it could, if experienced, be misunderstood as Void or NonBeing, also Darkness. In terms of The War in Heaven, this realm and the existences natural to it are the "Place" and the "UrGods" of Evil, working with absolute intensity toward the transformation of Cosmos into Chaos. To human reasoning, the fact of such "Forces" itself implies a kind of order. But that is not true, and the "order" is a fabrication of minds which cannot grasp the mystery.

Primordially contiguous to Chaos is Cosmos, the "Place" and "Forces" of Order, Good, "Light," Creative Harmony, and the Cosmic UrGods. Implacable as Chaos, Cosmos unwaveringly and with absolute intensity pursues the goal of transformation. Cosmos and Chaos are of the same degree of subtlety and only their subtle substance is completely and eternally real. Yet it is *as if* there have come to be, in a "space" between Cosmos and Chaos, dimensions of Being which most fundamentally are the arenas of conflict in which the struggles of the Forces take place. These arenas, and conflicts and combatants, have substance of varying degrees of subtlety, but more fundamentally they are appearances, imaginal constructs, functional representations of the essentially irrepresentable Powers and Principalities. The so-called "material" and "spiritual" worlds, including humans and their world(s), are such appearances and representations—something like "particles of mind," temporarily given differing kinds of existence and, in some instances, degrees of autonomy. These mysteries also go beyond human understanding, although Mystery Schools can impart a measure of understanding. What is important to really know and to fully believe is that man and his world(s) are not at all what they seem to be; that the apparent reality is far more malleable and subject to directed transformation than we are taught that it is or it seems to be; and that those belief systems which sustain such illusions as immutability and objectivity are also subject to alteration, *all* "Laws of Nature" amongst them.

"Above" Chaos is the created and already-imaginal realm of the Demonic Metaeidolons: Evil Gods, Demons, and other Chaotic entities. Correspondingly, "below" Cosmos is the realm of the Divine Metaeidolons: Gods and Goddesses, angels, demons, and others. This realm, too, is created and imaginal, and it is the Metaeidolons, whether of Cosmos or Chaos, which interact directly with the human dimensions. A few—the most potent—of these great Metaeidolons *represent* the UrGods of the two primordial realities.

"Above" the realm of the Metaeidolons of Chaos is the disordered "material" realm of the "subatomic particles," "matter" with chaotic, not just unpredictable, positions and velocities. This is the reality which is referred to by the second law of thermodynamics, predictive of the eventual triumph of Chaos. Similarly, "below" the realms of the Metaeidolons of Cosmos, there is the realm of "spirit," and equally potent and seemingly irrefutable "laws" of teleology predictive of evolution of consciousness and eventual transformation of "matter" into "spirit." It is also, however, an imaginal realm, without true immutable laws and is part of the transient, created arena, the "space" between Cosmos and Chaos. It is also called the realm of Evolutionary Order.

Next, limiting discussion to humans and their world(s), there are five human realities, each of them potentially knowable by man, who is able to participate in them by means of the five bodies he/she possesses. These are the "gross" and "subtle" bodies encountered in all major spiritual traditions and systems of magic and occultism.

The understanding of them is distorted, however, and some systems, for example, subcategorize, while others lump together, thus arriving at three, seven, nine, or some other number of bodies and their respective realities. The five human dimensions or worlds are a "midpoint" between the realities of chaotic "matter" and evolutionary "spirit."

The "gross material or physical body," or just "physical body" (AUFU), is the body of anatomy and physiology, and it is what most people think they mean by "my body." This body, however, has a brain but no mind and is therefore *not* the body of most experience, as will be explained more fully later. The second, more subtle body is the Double (KA), and it is the body usually experienced by the mind of that body; it is a *body image,* coincides more or less with the AUFU, and its sensations also are images or, more precisely, symbolic representations of an imaginal reality, which it in many ways distorts. This distortion is recognized by psychology so that some authors speak, for example, of a "symbolic coding" of the "actual" reality done by the brain or the brain-mind. Quite apart from metaphysics, one can accept that the *experience* of one's own and other bodies is not immediate but mediated by the mind, and "occurs in" the mind (or brain, if one chooses to regard mind as "epiphenomenon of brain").

As the KA's world is more subtle than the AUFU's, similarly the third body and world of the Shadow (HAIDIT) is more subtle than that of the KA. This is a reality ordinarily experienced as altogether "mental" and mostly "unconscious," the world, for example, of most dreams and most images experienced in trance and drug states. It can be a world of either the personal or the collective or transpersonal unconscious, a world that is the source of many works of art and which figures also in other sorts of "creativity." Many fail to consider that in, say, the dream world they have a body which is not the body of everyday experience and that the dream world also is a different reality, the dream body and dream worlds being unfettered by many of the "laws" which bind the world of the ordinary waking consciousness. As is true of the KA and the other subtle bodies, the HAIDIT is part of and interactive with that constellation of five bodies which is the human being. Therefore, its experiences can affect the others, particularly those inferior to it in subtlety, but the *more* subtle bodies also. Such interactions are most strikingly apparent in cases where the unconscious is clearly in a causal relationship to the sickness or healing of the physical body or the mind. Once again, this world of experience is well known to psychology. What is not grasped sufficiently, however, is that the world of the HAIDIT, or Shadow, is equally as real as the "objective" world, that the body of the HAIDIT is also equally real, and that the failure to recognize these facts is damaging and severely limiting.

The Magical Body and its world, or KHU, are only rarely consciously experienced but shape importantly that "work of art" or "myth" which the HAIDIT in its *own* consciousness *lives*, and which it imposes on the KA, which in turn lives out the same myth, but almost always unconsciously. These subtler realities, then, very largely determine the fate of the AUFU, including, accidents apart, when and how it will deteriorate and die. In ancient times when such matters were better understood, the KHU was not thought of as "magical," but as magico-spiritual, the line between magic and religion being artificial and imposed on human thinking by religions which already had lost much of their awareness and potency. The KHU was the "second order" reality and work of the magician-priest—only later, just of the magician. To live and act consciously in the KHU it is necessary to undergo a prolonged and very rigorous training. There are brief, spontaneous experiences of it, most often triggered by unusual stress and a resultant alteration of consciousness. Also, in some more primitive societies, shamans, witch doctors and similar figures still attain to fragmentary knowledge of the KHU and thus can generate some "paranormal" effects, but these fall far short of what is possible. Nevertheless, the importance of the KHU, which can serve either Cosmos or Chaos, is very great. Functioning unconsciously insofar as the less subtle bodies are concerned, it affects them and their worlds quite apart from determining the myth that is lived out. Each person is to some extent an "unconscious magician," affecting his world, including other persons, by telepathic, psychokinetic and other means. In some cases this "unconscious magic" can be extremely potent.

The "highest" and most subtle body and world is the SÂHU, or Spiritual Body, which again, more appropriately, should be magico-spiritual, but of the "first order." This is the world of authentic "religious experience" as it is attained to by rigorous practitioners of "spiritual disciplines"—"holy men," "saints," "spiritual masters," whatever they may be called in a particular system. In the ancient traditions, the high magician-priest was expected to be able to experience and work with the realities of both KHU and SÂHU. Presently, however, spiritual disciplines largely eschew the magical reality, aiming only at passive consciousness of the "spiritual" one—more rarely, spiritual Work and *interactions* with *Neters*. This limitation is crippling for spiritual development. And the true goal must be "complete" consciousness—that is, the knowledge and use of all five of the bodies and their respective dimensions. Similarly, the magician is crippled if his/her consciousness and Work do not extend beyond the KHU.

The SÂHU is the only human reality which is "congenial" to the Cosmic "Gods," although such Beings may "descend" all the way into the realm of the AUFU, which, however, is excremental to them. The "Gods" of Chaos ordinarily "ascend" only to the realm of the KHU, when a "black magic" is practiced. However, some of the most potent sometimes invade the SÂHU so that even the holiest of men or women is not secure from them. Also, the most powerful of black magicians can work with Metaeidolons representing the Ur-Gods of Chaos at this level, thus effecting the most potent evil.

Having now, in one possible way, summarized the background against which the human drama is played, my discussion will hereafter be limited to the human realities—the five bodies of man, the dimensions appropriate to each of those bodies, and the functional metapsychology which can be effectively worked with once their existences have been made known. However, before examining more completely the "gross physical body" and its place in the metapsychology, something needs to be said about the animation of the body and certain other elements which are required if it is to be human.

In addition to the five bodies, the human being has also two "spirits." One of these is commonly referred to as the Soul (BA) and, like the bodies, it is an arena in which the great opposing forces contend—in a larger way, but also for control of the person's bodies and his/her life. The BA is imperishable, or almost so, unlike the other "spirit," the SOKHIM, which dies along with the physical body and is a kind of foundation for consciousness, a link between body and mind. At birth the five bodies and the two spirits coalesce, a process that begins at the moment of conception but only is completed at the time of the physical birth. Also, at conception, the Breath of Life, or SA, must be released and enter in. It is this SA, or Life Force, that the Gods can draw upon for immortality. When a God chooses to die, he can do so by abstaining from a periodically needed assimilation of the SA. A human who gains access to the SA by magical means can use it to extend his/her own life. And when a human being of special gifts is conceived—one especially destined to serve Cosmos or Chaos—forces will contend to ensure or to prevent the infusion of SA, even though that occurs in the barest instant after fertilization. Cosmos and Chaos designate many more such intended children of destiny than ever effectively reach the world: either the SA infusion is blocked, the infant is destroyed in the womb or at birth, or the person may be removed at any time later on, whenever he/she is vulnerable. Despite attempts at protection, it is very rare that such gifted and chosen humans survive to carry out the Work assigned to them. Cosmos and Chaos are equally merciless in their efforts to eliminate the designates, since even one such person can drastically affect the human race.

AUFU:
THE "PHYSICAL BODY"

The AUFU, as mentioned, is the "physical body," with its muscles and bones, blood and internal organs, glandular and nervous systems—the body that anatomists and physiologists describe. Of itself it is a mechanical thing, a machine which, for all its awesome potentials, is propelled by mechanical functions, instincts, biological drives, sensations, and a limited number of learned responses and behaviors. It is operated by the brain and nervous systems, and for it to exist and be alive only minimal brain functions and a brain of very small size would be required. This body is "human" only by virtue of its unnecessarily large and, for it, quite superfluously complex brain—and, of course, its links with the four subtler bodies and souls. The AUFU lacks consciousness in any higher sense of the word, and its functioning is meaningful only to the mind of the KA, which (without special re-education) misinterprets it as its own behaviors, thoughts and feelings. The AUFU can sense, and it feels pain and pleasure, but its sensing and feeling are so distorted by the KA, which transmutes them into its own images, that their actuality is rarely any major portion of the contents of consciousness. The AUFU is thus falsified by the KA, which in turn is misled into thinking that it freely governs the "voluntary" functions and actions of the AUFU. This situation can be remedied only if by appropriate and strenuous means the KA is taught to differentiate itself from the

13

AUFU and also attains to a sufficiently accurate sensing, internal as well as surface, of the physical body.

All of the subtler bodies, and their minds, have powerful effects upon the AUFU. Their experiences can affect every part of it, and those experiences, when very vivid or prolonged, are not distinguished by the brain from the realities of its own world. The brain then brings about changes in parts and functions of the body as if these were responses to the body's own experiences.

The HAIDIT, or Shadow, is the only subtle body-mind which naturally possesses a good contact with and knowledge of the AUFU—meaning it can positively or negatively affect the physical body with equal facility. The KA once had such contact and capacity, but it has long since been lost. The Shadow can be understood as being roughly what is usually meant by "the unconscious," and appeals can be made to it to alter the AUFU along desired lines. An example of this would be to hypnotize the KA, so establishing contact with the HAIDIT, and then suggest to it that it utilize its special knowledge and relation to the body to, say, dispose of a wart or a tumor, or to increase or decrease blood flow to a particular part. Most effective hypnosis is a dialogue between the hypnotist and the Shadow, aimed at achieving certain changes in the AUFU, the KA, or the HAIDIT itself.

The mindless AUFU cannot effectively survive in the contemporary world and must minimally be tended and cared for by the KA or, if the personal KA is too feeble or deranged, by other persons. However, although it is a machine, even the most ordinary of these has unused potentials which are enormous and far in excess of what can be made use of by even the most developed and most knowledgeable person. Since it is essential to the life of the whole person, reason would dictate that it be well cared for and efforts made to use it well. However, the KA and the HAIDIT frequently behave towards it as if the AUFU were their mortal enemy; also, as if it were unworthy of being brought into the kind of awareness that would allow its potentials to be much better used.

The AUFU, especially its brain, is the essential foundation upon which rests the structure of the whole person, whatever his or her powers may be. Yet it is always in varying degrees badly fed, poorly exercised, little known, and inadequately used, while, at the same time, it is subjected to abuses which, if done to someone else, would constitute torture and deliberate destruction. No human being can be found who dies a natural death in the sense that his body parts wear out uniformly. The man who dies "naturally" is self-destroyed, killing himself by means of (barely) conscious behaviors which are largely products of unconscious processes and non-human forces.

The ancient Egyptians, as depicted in their paintings and sculptures, are the only known civilized people displaying an adequate knowledge of and regard for the healthy and well-functioning physical body. The bodies they almost universally depict are graceful and light, well-positioned in gravity, able to make use of directed energies which give access to strength in the absence of excessive muscular development. Obviously, the body image is intact, awareness of body mechanics is present, and mind and body are in harmonious, mutually supportive interaction. Already with the Greeks and in the ancient Far East, although to a lesser degree, art tells us that some of these elements were lost or were never present in the first place. With the Egyptians, AUFU and KA are differentiated in awareness, integrated in function. Moreover, with them the HAIDIT was in a superior, though far from perfected, relation to both AUFU and KA. Add to this the knowledge and awareness of some persons of the higher subtle bodies as well, making possible interaction with the *Neters,* and one uncovers basic secrets as to why the Egyptian civilization lasted so long and produced so much that even today is unrivaled.

The AUFU is a machine operated by its brain under the influence of the subtle bodies and their minds, but it is also a machine with a brain that is influenced from within its own and subtle bodies by the nonhuman forces of Cosmos and Chaos. These entities are "in" all of the bodies, although as the bodies become more subtle they tend to be less congenial to Chaos and more congenial to Cosmos. At the levels of AUFU and KA, however, the Chaotic entities preponderate, unless they have been exorcised or those bodies "seeded" with a greater number of their Cosmic antagonists— magico-spiritual operations which are a part of the Work on Oneself at the conscious KHU and SÂHU levels. In the HAIDIT, the antagonistic forces are, in most persons, better balanced—so that it is the arena of the greatest conflict. This is the "middle ground," and on the "higher ground" of KHU and SÂHU the balance shifts towards Order.

Because of the potency of the demons in the "gross" AUFU, it always sickens and dies much earlier than it might do otherwise. Even conscious Work by the KHU and the SÂHU can only delay for a time this outcome. For the same reason—demonic dominance— the KA, which survives the AUFU, rather quickly degenerates.

The Egyptians labored mightily to prevent this degeneration of the KA, but their efforts could at best delay it. Chaos, in the AUFU, works incessantly to achieve its debilitation and death, which Cosmos opposes. So long as humans remain at the level of the mechanical AUFU and sleepwalking KA, just so long will they remain destructive to themselves and to both their "subjective" and "objective" realities. To "awaken"—a major goal of every magical, spiritual, or magico-spiritual system—is to break through and out of that level of nonawareness at which one's life is determined through the body's misuse by the unconscious. Even awareness and intelligent use of AUFU, KA and HAIDIT would effect the most remarkable positive changes in humankind. The fulfillment of humanity's potential, however, implies an aware participation also by KHU and SÂHU bodies integrated with the others.

KA:
THE BODY OF EXPERIENCE

The term KA, or Double, is instructive. It informs us that the body of the KA should as closely as possible duplicate the AUFU so that the body image does not falsify the physical body for the mind—a falsification which, through their interactions, results in harm to both. At the same time, the KA must be aware that its body is *not* the body of the AUFU—the KA is *mind*, and its subtle body is a mental body and the only body it will experience. Nonetheless, it is also a *Double* so that to the extent it acquires self-knowledge which is accurate, it also accurately knows the physical body. The KA can attain to such self-awareness, and thus a knowledge of the AUFU, only by means of self-exploration. Existing psychophysical methods are available and of great help in such an undertaking.

The KA possesses many capacities it shares with the other subtle bodies, but not with the AUFU. By cultivating these, and by learning, it provides essential tools and information which the other bodies can and will make use of. If, on the other hand, it does not develop itself and learns inadequately, then the "higher" bodies will be crippled in their dealings with the KA's reality and otherwise as well. The KA possesses, most importantly, intellect, imagination, will, and the ability to assimilate and integrate knowledge. As the AUFU is basically affected by food, its environment, and its mechanical use, so the KA is affected by similar factors but has the

19

ability, wanting in the AUFU, to take some charge of its own development. It can also initiate better contact with the HAIDIT, "making conscious the unconscious," or part of it, which actually means integrating itself with the HAIDIT body-mind. This is as equally necessary a task for the KA as is its pursuit of knowledge of itself to gain knowledge of the AUFU. Both efforts, when successful, greatly strengthen the KA and give it a much larger autonomy. More importantly, they are the means to the integration of AUFU, KA and HAIDIT.

The "making conscious of (parts of) the unconscious" and the "exploration of the unconscious," which must be undertaken by the KA, means that the KA must learn to temporarily inhibit almost all of its own mental processes and allow its own field of consciousness to be occupied, as it were, by that of the HAIDIT. The KA must become a detached observer of the HAIDIT's world.

Just as the KA must come to understand that its body is not that of the AUFU, so must this typically egocentric KA understand that its mind is not that of the HAIDIT, another error to which it is prone. Neither must the KA suppose that the HAIDIT'S world and experiences are its world and experiences. Only if the KA thus differentiates and detaches itself can it safely undertake the exploration. Otherwise it may lose its grasp on its own world, and the KA also will give to the beings of the HAIDIT's world a power over it which the detachment and differentiation would prevent. If the KA, however, avoids such mistakes, it can expand and further liberate itself by making use of the *memories* which it brings back from the HAIDIT and then integrates into its own knowledge and understandings.

When the KA has attained to awareness of its body, and by that means to a knowledge of the AUFU, then it diminishes the power of the body to determine the contents and processes of the KA's mind. Similarly, by gaining knowledge of the HAIDIT, the KA diminishes the power of the unconscious to determine the contents and processes of its mind. This is of major importance to the *person* when the bodies have not yet been integrated. After integration, the more subtle HAIDIT "uses" the KA within the context of that higher unity within which AUFU, KA and HAIDIT have become effectively one.

By all of the subtle bodies *imagination* is used as a psychosensory system, and when working as it should, this system gives a symbolic but functionally accurate and effective rendering of the body and its world. In the case of the three highest subtle bodies,

imagination is also creative, and for the KHU and the SÂHU imagination gives knowledge of the magico-spiritual realms—becomes a
psychospiritual *and* psychosensory system. In the KA, however,
imagination is psychosensory only, serving to represent to the KA
its reality, which more or less coincides with the AUFU's. That aspect of imagination, which in the case of the more subtle bodies is
creative, in the KA yields only *fantasy*, something despised and
strongly warned against by esoteric traditions. For the KA, fantasy
is, at best, wasteful, and often it is more seriously damaging. Fantasy bodies are created which the KA and the AUFU then may mistake for their own. And the KA is impeded in its other major task,
which is that of knowing truly its own mind.

The KA must gain knowledge of its body and, thereby, the
AUFU's; and it must differentiate itself from the unconscious. But it
must also come to know its own mind, and for this it is necessary to
participate in work which does not always offer immediate rewards. It involves self-observation, concentration, strengthening
the tools of the mind and controlling its customary aimless mean-
derings and fantasies. The mind must be provided, and come to demand, its own proper foods and environments. In the ancient Mystery Schools, care was taken that this Work was made as interesting
and rewarding as possible. Nonetheless, most candidates fell away
here, lacking discipline to continue. But the mind of the KA must be
strengthened in its world in order to give some of the necessary
powers to the other subtle bodies. The KA of the person who has
chosen this Way must approach, within the KA's limits to do so, the
ideal of "sound mind in sound body." If it fails, the person can advance no further and, in the words of Gurdjieff, in the end will die
like a dog.

That is not a good comparizons considering that many dogs are more sensitive and loving than humans?

HAIDIT:
ON THE WAY OF THE
FIVE BODIES

The HAIDIT or Shadow can (roughly) be identified with what presently we call "the unconscious," including (some of) the "collective unconscious." It is the body with which the unconscious is experienced and the unconscious is its world. The term *Shadow* properly suggests that in these realities one is coming closer to the human dimension *noumena*—that the HAIDIT's world, or parts of it, is that of the "shadows" cast by more essential realities. This is unlike the world of the AUFU and the KA, which remain closed off from any direct knowledge of essential or higher realities, although they are affected by them.

The HAIDIT of the person on the Way has the primary task of differentiating itself from the "lower" bodies while, at the same time, functionally integrating itself with them. This is always what is meant by *integration,* and it should never be thought that a "higher" body or consciousness assimilates the others. Obviously, they continue to exist, but the interactions of the bodies and their minds are less conflicting as they become more unified. If the person experiences him- or herself as an "expanded consciousness," having access to unconscious processes, then there has been no true integration: simultaneous awareness of the three bodies is the criterion.

Were it not for the opposing nonhuman forces in humanity, a

23

near-total harmony of the authentically integrated bodies could be established. But neither Chaos nor Cosmos can accept a unification leaving one or the other powerless, and thus a complete absence of conflict and unwanted interactions between the three bodies is an ideal never realized.

The HAIDIT can "see into" and otherwise "sense into" the body of the AUFU and its Double, as well as sensing them from outside. Its own body is very largely self-created, although its choices about this are far from being free. Thus, it can imitate and fabricate for itself a body which grossly resembles the AUFU's and, less authentically still, it is able to create approximations to the AUFU's world—both as it actually is, and as it is known to the KA. The HAIDIT can also create for itself other bodies, taking any form it can imagine. Similarly, it is able to create any world it is able to imagine, and experience that world very fully. It is what the KA calls an "artist," although it "creates" as a natural part of its functioning—as, say, the AUFU breathes, senses, or excretes. The HAIDIT is hedonistic and, unless the KA's will has been highly developed, the HAIDIT's will is feeble, rendering its consciousness suggestible. The HAIDIT is, however, far from being just irrational and its mental powers potentially far exceed those of the KA.

The HAIDIT can best be reached and worked with by altering the consciousness of the KA so that it no longer is experienced and, seemingly, ceases to function. When the KA is thus "out of the way," then the personal field of consciousness is occupied by the HAIDIT, which can be dialogued with directly, guided and taught. It can then be directed to undertake that Work on itself which needs to be done before the HAIDIT can know itself and its world sufficiently to function as a part of an integrated, larger whole—that is, a more fully conscious person.

On the Way, the HAIDIT's guide or teacher supervises a prolonged, "expanding" and "deepening" exploration of the unconscious in which the HAIDIT, unlike the KA in its exploration, is an active participant, only seldom taking just a spectator role. The HAIDIT is taught to "manipulate time" so that in its world weeks, months and even years of exploration and other work can be accomplished during what are only minutes in the clock-measured world of the KA. Even so, the unconscious is so vast, and there is so much work to be done, that the effort usually takes years of KA-time to complete.

The HAIDIT, as explorer, maps the terrain, experiences and classifies the "flora and fauna," and otherwise expands its knowledge of its world—a world not only vast but incredibly diverse—learning to function in many different ways and in many different situations. It is gradually exposed to experiences which, at the start, would have been unendurable for it, and which usually it manages to avoid when left unguided. Since extreme pleasures are available in its world, the HAIDIT is led to experience these to a degree and in ways which it rarely would have been able to discover for itself since, typically, the HAIDIT is too "lazy" to venture into the deeps and extremities of the Shadow world. It is satisfied with the blander pleasures near the surface and center of its world, and thus also avoids the graver dangers. The pleasures it is given are rewards for its efforts and compensate for fear and pain it also must experience. The guide must maintain the hedonistic HAIDIT's motivation by seeing to it that the pleasures outweigh the negative experiences. Eventually, the HAIDIT must confront what previously would have led to panic, madness, even death.

Some of this exploration coincides with the KA's development of *its* mind. It must be done before the KA's will has been strengthened to the point that the HAIDIT is affected and rendered insufficiently suggestible. A delicate balance needs to be maintained so that the HAIDIT develops its own will and learns to use its other mental powers, unimpeded by changes in the KA. When the HAIDIT's will and other little-used potentials are strong enough, then the work with the KA can be completed. The HAIDIT will then, if the work was done correctly, voluntarily or willingly cooperate in further exploration and self-development.

In addition to exploring parts of the unconscious—by no means all, but enough to allow Work at the "higher" level of the KHU—and in addition to developing its will and learning to make use of other mental faculties, the HAIDIT is taught to use its powers to function constructively in its interactions with the AUFU and the KA. It especially is taught how not to introduce conflicts and confusion into the conscious mind, and how not to generate negative effects in the physical body. The HAIDIT also learns how to join in cooperative problem solving with the KA, thus making the KA "more creative and more intelligent," and it learns to bring about healing and other beneficial changes in both KA and AUFU. The ability of the unconscious to intervene in these ways in the workings of the

conscious mind, and to alter the body for good or ill, is well established. It does so continuously and is far more decisive in shaping
the life of the ordinary person than the conscious mind, apart from
it, ever is. But when "the unconscious has been made (partly) conscious" and the integration with the lower bodies is achieved, then
there is easier and still more potent interaction which becomes possible. Now, however, it can be *chosen* and intelligently *used*.

Finally, the HAIDIT, in its world, lives out a "myth" or a "work
of art" imposed on it from both within and without, which begins to
unfold during a person's childhood and continues until his/her
death. Sometimes the myth appears to change, but this is an illusion.
Only when there is integration with KHU, SÂHU, or both can the
person truly alter his/her myth, which it may or may not be desir-
able to do. This myth is the "meaning" of a person's life, and if made
known to him/her prematurely, can destroy his/her illusion of
autonomy and lead to hopelessness. The teacher will typically
know what the myth is long before the student knows it and must
decide when to disclose it to the student. It must be disclosed at
some point along the Way, but only when the student is ready and is
going to be able to change it if need be.

One part of the Work at the level of the KHU is to either choose
a new myth or choose to continue with the "given" one. Then, in
either case, there is some real, not illusory, freedom, and the work
aims towards a fuller realization of the myth and its constructive—
or destructive—potentials. The personal myth has a "guiding archetype," and, if the myth is to be altered, the archetype must be con-
fronted in the HAIDIT and often its symbolic form must be destroyed. If the Shadow attempts this battle without having access to
the powers of the KHU, it will almost inevitably fail and the person
will sustain severe, if not fatal, injury. However, if the archetype is
constructive so that the myth is also constructive, it can serve the
person as an ally and teacher in the HAIDIT and be safely and use-
fully worked with, as some psychological, occult and other approaches to human healing and development do or try to do. However, that the archetype is "constructive" does not mean that the
myth is worthy of the person—it still may need to be changed to allow his/her larger potentials to be realized.

The myth lived by the HAIDIT in its world determines the life
of the KA in its broad outlines and also in many of its details. It can
be deduced by observing the KA and directly observed by making

conscious the HAIDIT and learning how it functions in its world—its behaviors and experiences. But, again, in most cases the myth should remain concealed from the person until he/she is ready to experience the KHU and its world: until then, it is unalterable.

The person is ready for the KHU-level Work when his/her awareness differentiates—simultaneously and with functional integration—the physical body, the conscious mind and the unconscious—now itself sufficiently in consciousness.

KHU:
THE "MAGICAL BODY"

Those bodies—KHU and SÂHU—which are involved in true magico-religious Work can be thought of as the "higher unconscious," collective and personal. The "House of Life" of the ancient Egyptians and other Mystery Schools aimed at making these bodies conscious and integrating them with the "lower" bodies. The KHU was made conscious and its powers developed by means we now think of as "magical." The SÂHU was made conscious and its powers developed by what we now think of as religious or spiritual practices. (Actually it is a question of *emphasis* since for both KHU and SÂHU the work combines magical and spiritual elements.) When these higher bodies are made conscious, a person lives at once in two different realities: he/she acts in the mundane world of everyday life, and also interacts with the *Neters*, participating thereby in their supramundane world.

The world of the KHU is essentially a School and a Temple. One who has developed to this level of consciousness will, hereafter, have a *Neter*—"God" or "Goddess"—as his or her primary Teacher. If a human teacher has brought the person this far, that teacher may still assist in the Work but assumes a secondary role. The Teacher may also be assisted by other *Neters*—subordinates in the Way being taught. By means of his/her opened psychospiritual senses, accessible when the KHU is made conscious, the pupil is

29

able to participate fully in the realities created for him/her by the Teacher. The quality of his/her work will determine whether the KHU remains conscious. It is quite possible to "fail" in the School— then the higher consciousness is lost and the KHU world remains in the mind only as a wondrous memory.

True ritual and ceremonial magic, involving elaborate and potent symbol systems; HEKAU (Words of Power); consciousness-altering sounds, gestures, postures and Sacred Movements; means of activating centers and energy systems of the subtle bodies; subtle body diagnosis and healing; methods of attack and defense; metamorphosis and transformation of the bodies; psychospiritual alchemy; philosophy and theology of Cosmos and Chaos; and ways of interacting with the *Neters*—these are aimed at developing the KHU and enabling it to use its capacities.

The magician is taught and learns to function, first of all, exclusively in the KHU world and the KHU body. Later, however, the "whole person" (SÂHU, at this level of the Work, excepted) participates—so that, for example, the Sacred Movements, gestures and postures are executed by the four bodies simultaneously. This furthers integration of the bodies and also makes the work more effective in the worlds of the less subtle bodies. The postures, movements, and some other procedures are also used to help lower-level students advance to the higher states of consciousness. In Yoga, for example, consciousness is directed to centers (*chakras*) found only in the KHU and SÂHU bodies in the hope that this will activate the subtle centers—a procedure which bears little fruit. The Yoga postures (*asanas*) are more efficacious and lay a foundation for higher development. But Yoga, for all its merits, unfortunately survives only in fragments; too much is missing, and the psychophysical methods of the Way are a more complete approach to mind-body integration and awareness. Moreover, most Yoga teaching professes a bias against *siddhis*—precisely those powers which the KHU must acquire and develop to realize itself and to do its appropriate Work, including preparation for integrating KHU and SÂHU. Like other present-day spiritual disciplines, Yoga is focused on attaining to those states of consciousness available at the SÂHU level—*Samadhi, Nirvana* and others—and, at best, only realizes approximations to these since the level of the KHU is inadequately worked with. These disciplines also have forgotten that the *siddhis*, subject to abuse in the mundane realities, are essential tools for the *most* important Work—interaction with the *Neters* and participation in The War in Heaven. Similarly, such "states" as Nirvana, Samadhi, Cosmic Consciousness, Enlightenment, are but means by which the SÂHU is strengthened to do its greater Work.

The KHU's "magic" and the SÂHU's "spiritual practices" are simply psychological, psychophysical and psychospiritual methods applicable at "levels of consciousness" which ordinary psychologies and other modern approaches fail to deal with and typically believe not to exist. Just as many people do not believe in the incredible wealth of the unconscious, until they experience it in trance or drug states, so there is a disbelief in the still more remote and higher reaches of the unconscious until, by appropriate means, these too can be experienced. The disbelief is merely a product of ignorance based upon lack of first-hand experience. The Work with the KHU makes plain its reality and further enlarges and expands one's awareness of what *is*. Until this is done, the person is cut off and alienated from his/her own Higher Self and potentials and, whatever his/her other attainments, is for practical purposes "spiritually dead."

The person who has integrated physical body, conscious mind and the (HAIDIT) unconscious already has advanced far enough to be greatly differentiated from less developed human beings. His/her life will almost certainly be rich and productive and he/she will live in close enough proximity to the higher realities that there will be no fear of actual spiritual death or of life losing its meaning. This is not true, sad to say, of the majority of humankind.

When there has been no effective Work at all—no integration of body and mind, no exploration of the unconscious—then the "person" sleepwalks through life and is "human" only in form and potential. In practical fact, he/she is humanoid only, a mechanical unit having just the appearance of a "human." If one looked into his/her unrealized potentials, then one would see that the world of the KHU is silent and unmoving, as if lifeless. The KHU body lies inert and sleeping as it dreams the essence of the myth that is the "meaning of life" for that person. The Temple and its School stand empty except for this body and what appear to be statues representing certain Gods and other beings. This is the latent and waiting world and body of the person who is cognitively cut off from the higher realities and "spiritual" Forces. The KHU body and world can come intensely and vibrantly—numinously and awe-fully—

alive, but only if "brought to life" by Work. Otherwise the *Neters*, who might have been the Teachers, remain only statuesque representations; the Temple and the School remain forever silent as a tomb. If all Work on the less subtle bodies is neglected, and if they should be sufficiently misused, then the person does spiritually die and the KHU no longer even dreams the essence of the myth. With that, the meaning of life is lost altogether and there is an inner void far more terrible even than the living of an inane and destructive myth. More, that same life may have to be lived over and over. This is what Gurdjieff, many of whose teachings had their roots in those of ancient Egypt, meant when he said that the person who fails to do the Work on Oneself will perish like a dog. ⸙

SÂHU:
THE "SPIRITUAL BODY"

· The SÂHU'S world exists in closest proximity to the world of the *Neters*—more exactly, to the realms of the Evolutionary Order, or "Spirit," and of the Divine Metaeidolons, representations of the Gods and UrGods of Cosmos. The "black" magician, by means of his magic, reverses this positioning of bodies and worlds so that his own SÂHU world is in proximity to the realms of Disordered Matter and the Demonic Metaeidolons, representations of the Evil Gods of Chaos. Thus, there can occur the most complete interactions between the SÂHU magician-priests or -priestesses and the respective Forces which they serve.

In The Way of the Five Bodies, the *Neters* interacted with directly at KHU- and SÂHU-level are the Goddess Sekhmet and The Eight (Gods and Goddesses) associated with Sekhmet, as well as the demigods, demons and other entities. The antagonist is Set, UrGod of Chaos, and Set's associated Powers and Principalities. Some of these Forces contend in each of the human dimensions, and they are always present in body and mind, personality and essence, of every individual. Only at the higher levels of awareness and Work can they be known to some extent for what they are, can be differentiated from one's own psychophysical and psychospiritual self, and be allied with or opposed.

The *Neters*, through their representations, reveal themselves

35

only gradually, first to the KHU and then to the SÂHU body and its imaginal senses and consciousness. The human must be sufficiently prepared for such contact with the self-declared *Other*, strengthened and otherwise made ready by progressive Work cumulatively affecting every part and aspect of his/her being. There can be brief, approximate experiences of the higher realities in the absence of such preparation. Many people are given "intimations" and, for them, powerful experiences of the Forces with which KHU and SÂHU do their Work—examples of "incursions," "paranormal phenomena" sufficient to call into question the "consensual reality" and the "Grace" of religious experience—these are "reminders" of a *Something Beyond* the ordinary world, and "lures" which beckon and sometimes impel towards cognition of that at which they hint or which they flashingly disclose. But the undeveloped person could never endure the continuous occurrence and numinous qualities of such manifestations as a part of the Work of the KHU and the SÂHU—the intensity and range of energies, feelings, overpowering Otherness, preternatural beauty and grisly horror—in the uncanny and awe-ful dread-allure of the love-wrath and other aspects of the Presence of the *Neters*.

The KHU, when its Work is sufficiently advanced, receives an initiation and performs operations to make the SÂHU conscious. The SÂHU's Work differentiates it from the KHU and the other bodies and it becomes functionally integrated with them. Then the "highest" Work can be accomplished in each of the five human dimensions—the realms of the Five Bodies. Not that the Work is ever completed, or the human potentials ever made fully accessible, but there is an approximation to the ideal which exceeds what could be accomplished by means of any lesser effort. Not just decades, but centuries of Work by the integrated Five Bodies would be needed to completely actualize and *master* the richness of a human being's potentials.

The SÂHU continues much of the Work begun by the KHU and adds to this other Work which the KHU could not have done. This "Spiritual Body" is, above all, an adept of self-regulated "movement" along the continuum of consciousness, becoming eventually able to experience states of consciousness which otherwise can only be *given* by the *Neters*. Foremost among these is what some schools call *Kundalini*, an "energy system" which, in the Egyptian metapsychology, is identified with the Goddess Sekhmet. By "raising

Kundalini"—which only the SÂHU can do, although lower bodies counterfeit the experience—the brain of the physical body is altered and much more of it comes into use, increasing the powers of all the bodies. Then the SÂHU, if proper Work is done, can acquire SEK-HEM (Power or Might). SEKHEM is the most formidable of the human potentials and allows its conscious possessor to function both in the human dimension and in the interaction with *Neters* in ways that would, if they were known, appear "superhuman" to non-initiates.

The SÂHU body, when not deliberately altered, is transparent and luminous so that its symbolic centers and energy systems can be clearly seen. Like its world, it is of the subtlest substance to be found in the dimensions of the human, and thus the Soul (BA) is in the SÂHU body. This extreme subtlety allows the SÂHU to be dissolved into, and to merge with, the substance of its world. This is the authentic "mystical experience"—again there are counterfeits and approximations—which some religious and spiritual disciplines misinterpret as a merging with the Divine Substance, God, or Ground of Being. It is not that, but it is a powerful and sometimes tranformative experience. After "dissolution," the body may reorganize in a way that is superior to its previous organization, affecting not only just the SÂHU but one or more of the other bodies also. The authentic "mystical experience" is of itself beneficial and is one aspect of the psychospiritual alchemy practiced by KHU and SÂHU to the end that the radical transformation of the person is achieved—higher integration and greater subtlety in each of the "lower" bodies.

The SÂHU also self-directedly "moves" into other states of consciousness and realms of experience described in the literatures of various world religions. These include what we know as Samadhi, Nirvana, Satori, and many others which also strengthen the SÂHU and further both its Work "in the world" and with the *Neters*. Such experiences, when not misunderstood—not regarded, for example, as ends in themselves—give a larger perspective on reality, help to break down limiting belief systems, further the psychospiritual alchemical process, and yield other benefits. The efforts required to attain to these experiences do, however, expose the SÂHU, and the whole person, to suffering and dangers—at least some of which are unavoidable. The so-called "Dark Night of the Soul" and various other experiences of Dread, Despair, Confusion,

and sicknesses of body and mind (in one or more of the bodies, although in fact *not* in the Soul) are examples. Yet these too, assuming
they are overcome, will strengthen the person to "Stand at One
'Time' in Five Worlds."

The SÂHU can perceive, although not enter into, the nonhuman realms of Evolutionary Order and the Disordered Particles
and those of the Divine and Demonic Metaeidolons. KHU, and even
HAIDIT, are sometimes given "visions" of these, but the SÂHU can
choose to *perceive* them with all its senses and, interacting upon its
allegiance, strengthens its love for Cosmos or Chaos, and its abhor-
rence of the Antagonist, by means of its perceptions of them. We
speak of the SÂHU as doing these things when it has not as yet
achieved integration with the other four bodies. Subsequent to integration, it is the *person* who acts, although he/she does so still in one
or another of the human *dimensions*—in this case, the SÂHU world.
Despite the extravagant claims made by some religions, the human
being *never* goes beyond the human dimensions and could not survive contact even with the appearances or representations of the
Neters in their far more subtle worlds. To speak of direct and immediate knowledge of God or of the Divine is a gross absurdity and
born, at best, of ignorance and self-delusion.

After the differentiation/integration of the Five Bodies has
been finally achieved, the priest-magician or magician-priest continues learning and other Work, advancing through the Hierarchy
to whatever levels of initiation he/she will ultimately reach. He/she
may Work mainly "in the world," possibly as a Teacher, or in some
mundane position where his magico-spiritual powers can exert useful influence—business, politics, communications, whatever—or
he/she may Work almost entirely with the *Neters*, doing the so-
called "Inner Work." In any case, unless he/she be otherwise in-
structed, the magician-priest or -priestess will Work secretly. Those
close to the person may have some inkling of what he/she does, but
it will not be a "public" Work. An occasional Teacher or, far more
rarely, a designated *Exemplar* will be the sole exceptions. If human
beings were not "sleeping," they would recognize at once the person well-advanced in the Work. That they do not is a helpful safe-
guard which, however, it is the Work's purpose to remove.

The search for a real School and a KHU- or SÂHU-level
Teacher is made much more difficult by the fact that those advanced
in the Work do it quietly and almost always secretly. Further, there

are always many false claimants to the knowledge of the Work, and others who are so self-deluded that they actually suppose themselves to have the knowledge. For every Gurdjieff—the foremost authentic Teacher of this century—there are thousands of the others, and millions to believe them until their "teachings" are proved empty.

There are a few guidelines that can aid in recognizing real Teachers. Such a man or woman can be known, for example, by the *conscious* manner in which he or she lives out the profound and powerful "myth" or "work of art" *chosen*. (The criteria just mentioned would exclude such powerful but *somnambulistic* magicians as Adolf Hitler and Aleister Crowley.) The integration of the four (or five) bodies will invest the Teacher with recognizable *Presence* and *Force*. Even if one is only slightly self-observant, it can be recognized that one's consciousness alters when in contact with a Teacher. One is affected in a way that is obviously "different"; one may "go into trance," or "awaken," or experience other "altered states," and the Teacher will not, as others do, speak to the KA of a person, but rather to HAIDIT—not to the conscious mind, but rather to the unconscious. And the Teacher can also speak directly to the AUFU, to its brain and nervous systems, or to the physical body as a whole, thus producing important beneficial (or destructive) changes in it. This *is* Teaching; it gives pain as well as pleasure, forcing into consciousness various contents which had been repressed or otherwise excluded. It exposes limits to freedom and to growth, and it stirs a hunger for the "something more."

One can *give* some of these powers to false teachers, but at a cost to oneself that self-observation can detect. The authentic Teacher may "accept" or "take" power from others, but he/she, at the appropriate time, returns much more than was given and/or taken. One who meets such criteria *may* be a Teacher, but those who are "searching" should pursue the matter further. One must also find a way to determine whether it is Cosmos or Chaos that he/she serves, and choose according to one's predilection. Above all, do not expect "perfection," but heed that Scripture which says "it is nowhere to be found." The highly developed human being will be found to have large faults accompanying great virtues. This is inevitable in one who has become "larger than life." Nor should one expect "perfection" even from "the Gods," which would mean being foolish enough to "judge" such Beings as the *Neters* by human standards.

The Egyptian metapsychology, set forth in The Way of the Five Bodies, brings the aspirant to levels—those of KHU and SÂHU—where the Teaching is done not by humans but by the *Neters*, and primarily by the Goddess Sekhmet. As the Egyptians recognized, no human Teacher, however remarkable, can carry the Work into the Higher Realities where it can only be effective when done in interaction with Beings whose grasp extends beyond the human. There *are* other ways of making KHU or SÂHU, although not both, *partly* conscious and which thereby give *power*, sometimes formidable power. But the magical, occult or spiritual Path which stops short of effecting *working with* a Higher Force is inadequate. The person remains but a pawn in The War in Heaven and cannot effectively work for humanity's necessary transformation. He/she will lack essential protection and guidance and will commit many foolish and dangerous mistakes. For these reasons, the metapsychology speaks, with both compassion and harshness, of magical or spiritual disciplines done without the guidance of the *Neters* as "Paths of Fools."

CONCLUSION

The knowledgeable reader will be aware that what has been given in these pages sets forth with a most unusual completeness essentials of Work in a Mystery School. There are also many important details concerning magico-spiritual practices—*applications*—for those who can fill in between the lines. And enough has been said to allow a few persons, those of sufficient maturity, knowledge and daring, to *begin* the Work, even without School or Teacher. Thus, some of those might reach that condition where "When the pupil is ready, the Teacher will appear."

THE GODDESS SEKHMET

Among the most powerful of all the ancient Egyptian Deities was the Triad of Memphis—the Goddess Sekhmet and the Gods Ptah and Nefer-Tem. Memphis was the main site of the worship of the Triad and also of the House of Life, or Mystery School, where the powerful magico-religious systems associated with those Deities were taught. To the extent that this Knowledge survives, it is to be found in the Path or Way of the Goddess Sekhmet, known as THE WAY OF THE FIVE BODIES.

Ptah, brother and husband of Sekhmet, is often called simply the Creator God—the God who created the material world and who also, acting upon Sekhmet's urging, gave to human beings for their pleasure and as a means to self-realization the arts—literature, music, painting and sculpture, among others. The God Thoth is sometimes considered to be the intellect of Ptah, in which case Ptah also gave to humanity the sciences, mathematics and philosophy. Known as Father of Fathers, and Power of Powers, Ptah is said to have made his own body. He is usually represented as slender with a large, completely bald head and benign countenance.

Nefer-Tem, son of Sekhmet and Ptah, is also represented as human-bodied and slender, usually bearded and wearing one or another kind of elaborate headdress. He is the God who gave medicine to humans and thus is the God of Physicians—the God who eventually developed into the Greek Asclepius and who is still identified

43

with medicine today. In some representations of him, Nefer-Tem has the head of a lion, thus resembling his lioness-headed mother Sekhmet.

The Goddess Sekhmet is undoubtedly one of the most ancient Deities known to the human race—much older than Ptah, Her brother-husband, or Ra, Her father, the Sun God and King of the Gods. She came into Egypt from a place unknown and at a time unrecorded. Some of Her Names refer to this very great antiquity—Lady of the Place of the Beginning of Time, and One Who Was Before the Gods Were. As a form of the Great Mother, Sekhmet is also known as Mother of All the Gods.

Much is to be learned about Her from Her various Names and "Epithets," and some of those (originally four thousand) Names will be listed and discussed later. But they include, to mention just a few more, Lady of Flame, Great One of Magic, and Lady of the Lamp. The first of these titles refers to Her mastery of the sun's power, expressed by the solar disc with uraeus serpent usually worn on Her head. Great One of Magic acknowledges the awesome power attributed to Her priest-magicians. And Lady of the Lamp probably refers to the use of trance states by Her magician-priests and in the performance of Her Mysteries. Almost always the images of Sekhmet represent Her with the powerful but graceful body of a human female and head of a lioness.

The famed classical Egyptologist Sir Wallis Budge comments that the name Sekhmet has been derived from or is connected with the root *sekhem*—to be strong, mighty, violent. Others have added the meaning of sexual power, and it is believed that Sekhmet is the Goddess of the Kundalini energy constellation, discovery of which is often improperly attributed to Indian Tantra. Budge remarks that the meaning "strong, mighty, violent," would be appropriate to Sekhmet as She was the personification of the fierce, scorching and destroying heat of the sun's rays. He adds:

> In the form of the serpent goddess Mehenet, she took up her position on the head of her father Ra, and poured out from herself the blazing fire which scorched and consumed his enemies who came near, whilst at those who were some distance away she shot forth swift fiery darts which pierced through and through the fiends whom they struck. In a text quoted by Dr. Brugsch, she is made to say, "I set the fierce heat of the fire for a distance of millions of cubits between Osiris and his enemy, and I keep away from him the evil ones, and remove his foes from his habitation." One of the commonest names of the goddess is Nesert, i.e., Flame, as a destroying element, and in texts of all pe-

riods she plays the part of a power which protects the good and annihilates the wicked.

In the same place, Budge quotes a passage from the *EGYPTIAN BOOK OF THE DEAD*, of interest here because it enumerates various aspects and roles typical to this Goddess, even though here She is joined to Her father, Ra, and Her sister, the cat-headed Goddess Bast:

> Homage to thee, O Sekhmet-Bast-Ra, thou mistress of the gods, thou bearer of wings, thou lady of the red apparel, queen of the crowns of the South and North, Only One, sovereign of her father, superior to whom the gods cannot be, thou mighty one of enchantments (or, words of power) in the Boat of Millions of Years, thou who art preeminent, who risest in the seat of silence, mother of PASHAKASA, queen of PAREHAQA-KHEPERU, mistress and lady of the tomb, Mother in the horizon of heaven, gracious one, beloved, destroyer of rebellion, offerings are in thy grasp, and thou art standing in the boat of thy divine father to overthrow (the fiend) Qetu. Thou hast placed Maat in the bows of his boat. Thou art the fire goddess Ammiseshet, whose opportunity escapeth her not. . . . Praise be unto thee, O Lady, who art mightier than the gods, words of adoration rise unto thee from the Eight Gods of Hermopolis. The living souls who are in their hidden places praise the mystery of thee, O thou who art their mother, thou source from which they sprang, who makest for them a place in the hidden Underworld, who makest sound their bones and preservest them from terror, who makest them strong in the abode of everlastingness, who preserves them from the evil chamber of the souls of HES-HRA, who is among the company of the gods. Thy name is SEFI-PER-EM-HES-HRA-HAPU-TCHET-F.[1]

The views of most writers toward the Goddess Sekhmet—typically one imitating another—are negative, emphasizing Her destructiveness and tending to dwell almost exclusively upon a single myth or legend, one most often referred to as "The Myth of the Destruction of Mankind" by the Goddess Sekhmet. In this "myth," partly recorded by sculptures made on the walls of the tomb of Seti, humans entered into a conspiracy to overthrow the Gods. They blasphemed against Ra, king of Gods and men, and heretical priests and magicians plotted ways to turn against the Gods for their destruction, using those very powers the Gods had given to men that they might flourish and grow great upon the earth.

Ra, hearing of this plan, called to meet with him the most an-

cient and potent Deities, those who had been with him in the prime-
val waters before the time when with his eye, the sun, he had made
life. The Gods counseled together and it was decided that Sekhmet,
the force against which no other force avails, should manifest on the
earth and quell the rebellion. Sekhmet would manifest and punish
all those who had held in their minds evil images and imagined
wicked plots.

Then Sekhmet walked among men and destroyed them, and
drank their blood. Night after night Sekhmet waded in blood,
slaughtering humans, tearing and rending their bodies, and drinking their blood. The other Gods decided that the slaughter was
enough and should stop, but they could find no way to stop
Sekhmet, who was drunk on human blood.

As the carnage went on, the Gods recognized that Sekhmet,
Her rage sustained by intoxication, would implacably proceed with
the killing until the last human life had been extinguished. Then Ra
had brought to him from Elephantine certain plants which have
been said to be of the *Solanaceae* family and which can be brewed as
powerful mind-altering drugs. Those plants, and possibly also
opium or hemp, were sent to the God Sekti at Heliopolis. Sekti
added these drugs to a mixture of beer and also human blood, until
seven thousand great jugs of the substance had been made. The jars
were taken to a place where Sekhmet would pass and there were
poured out onto the ground, inundating the fields for a great distance. And when Sekhmet came to the fields and perceived what
She thought to be blood, She rejoiced and drank all of the liquid.
Then "Her heart was filled with joy," Her mind was changed, and
She thought no more of destroying mankind.

After that, Ra addressed Sekhmet as the One Who Comes in
Peace, praising the beauty and charm of the Goddess. The occasion
was afterwards celebrated among humans by a feast at which beautiful girls prepared a beverage containing the drugs which had been
administered to the Goddess. These girls, serving as priestesses of
Sekhmet, participated then with male celebrants in an orgiastic festival held in Sekhmet's honor. One of the most famous of these was
the festival held at Denderah in the Month of Thoth, and the most
important aspect of this gathering was the experience made possible by the drinking of the substance thought to be identical, save for
the human blood, with that prepared for Sekhmet by the Gods. Such
orgiastic festivals were also held after battles with the hope of paci-
fying the Goddess' more destructive nature. People danced, played,
and shook the sistrum, celebrating Sekhmet as "Beautiful," "Bril-

liant," and "Adorable" to soothe Her wildness. Sekhmet came eventually to represent the ecstasies of love.

There are some important passages dealing with the very great antiquity of Sekhmet in human religions to be found in the monumental work on ancient Egypt written by Gerald Massey, nineteenth-century scholar and trance visionary. Massey identifies Sekhmet as the Great Mother, Mother of Mystery, later denounced in the *Book of Revelation* as the Great Harlot:

> In Revelation, the mother of mystery is called "Babylon the Great, the mother of harlots and of abominations of the earth," who has the name of mystery written on her forehead (ch. xvii, 5). But there was an earlier Babylon in Egypt, known to the secret wisdom, which is traditionally identified with the locality of Coptos, nominally the seat of Kep, the Kamite mother of the mysteries. The mother of mystery did not originate with the scarlet woman of Babylon (nor as the red hag of the Protestants), although the title of the Great Harlot was applied to her also, who was the mother of harlots and to whom the maiden-tributes were religiously furnished in the city. Hers is a figure of unknown antiquity in the astronomical mythology, which was constellated as the red hippopotamus that preceded the Great Bear. The red hippopotamus (Apt) had already become the scarlet lady in the Ritual. Hence the Great Mother, as Sekhmet-Bast, who is higher than all the gods, and is the only one who stands above her father, is called *The Lady of the Scarlet-Coloured Garment* (Rit., ch. 164, Naville). The Kamite Constellation of the "birthplace" may also serve to show why the "great harlot" should have been so badly abused in the Book of Revelation. The creator of the Great Mother was depicted in the sign of the mesnhen to indicate the place of bringing forth by the cow of heaven whose "thigh" is the emblem of great magical power in the hieroglyphics. The mother of mystery also carries "in her hand a golden cup full of abominations, even the unclean things of her fornication."[2]

In another volume of the same work, Massey provides some related materials, drawing upon the same quotation from the *BOOK OF THE DEAD* cited earlier. Here, Massey notes:

> The Great Mother is saluted as the Supreme Being, the "Only One," by the name of Sekhmet-Bast, the goddess of sexual passion and strong drink, who is the mistress of the gods, not as wife, but as the promiscuous concubine—she who was "uncreated by the gods" and who is "mightier than the gods." To her the eight gods offer words of adoration. Therefore they

were not then merged in the Put-circle of the nine. It is
noticeable too that Sekhmet is not at that time saluted as the
consort of Ptah. Sekhmet was undoubtedly far more ancient
than Ptah... [3]

Newer religions attack older ones, transforming their gods into
devils and other debased forms, and it is not surprising that
Sekhmet, as the most ancient genetrix, is attacked as the Great Harlot. However, this is not to suggest that there is any infidelity to the
Egyptian Sekhmet in characterizing Her as a Goddess of powerful
sexual passions and with a love for intoxication states.

Sekhmet is Protectress of the Divine Order and, as such, protects the Gods against whatever evil forces may menace them. Fero-
cious though She is, Her power is never arbitrarily directed. Like the
lioness, She fiercely protects what She loves and that for which She
is responsible, destroying transgressors and other evildoers and
enemies of the Gods or of the Pharaoh. A Goddess of Wrath,
Sekhmet retaliates with total savagery whenever She or Her allies
are attacked or wronged in some way. But although She may seem
to welcome the opportunity to respond to aggression, there is no
evidence of Her ever initiating or provoking conflict. Her great
power to destroy is dedicated to righteous ends, and it is because of
Her power that morally correct but destructive tasks are made Hers.
Her reactions thus, no matter how violent, are essentially actions
stemming from loyalty and love.

The principal methods of destruction associated with the Goddess were fire, pestilence or plague, and drought. She was thought
to have Her primary dwelling place in the desert, where She loved
to roam in full lioness body, and would from there send hot winds
carrying disease and epidemics to destroy enemies. Memphis was,
as mentioned, the main site of Her religion, and places sacred to Her
were found throughout Egypt, but it was the desert where She
sought Her solitude. Bringer of diseases, Sekhmet also was the
Great One of Healing. Her magician-priests were the greatest of
healers and Her son, Nefer-Tem, the God of physicians. The same
dualism occurs with respect to Her role as Goddess of Fertility and
the One Who Controls the Waters of Life. Similarly, She is both Goddess of War and Goddess of Love. And, as the Flaming One, She had
the capacity to totally destroy subtle bodies and souls so that there
could be for the victim no afterlife, resurrection or reincarnation. Yet
Sekhmet was also the greatest protector of the dead in the Underworld.

The experience of the newly dead in the "Underworld" was an

important part of the Mysteries of Sekhmet, as it was of some other Egyptian Gods and Goddesses. Would-be initiates, in profound trances, experienced themselves as dying and going into the Underworld where much of what then befell them was believed by the Egyptians to be the same as what actually happens to the newly dead. One reason for this aspect of the Mysteries was to remove from the candidates the fear of death—the full realization of one's potentials, and satisfactory progression along the Way of the Goddess, being impossible until and unless such fear was excised. Some of the Underworld experiences of the "dead" candidate were of fiends and vampires and other horrors also believed to await the actually dead. Those who could not overcome their fear of these terrifying beings were "screened out" since the Path of the magician-priest would only result in madness, severe physical illness and possibly death for those who could not overcome their fear in the trance-death experiences. Those who did overcome fear of apparitions and eventually fear of death then could penetrate still deeper into the Mysteries and, perhaps, eventually achieve full status as magician-priest of Sekhmet.

The Goddess represents, and contains within Herself, that same enormously powerful energy called *Kundalini* in Tantric and some other Indian Traditions. Kundalini is the "coiled serpent" or feminine sexual energy which is in both men and women. It is called the *shakti*, or "power aspect," of the individual. To properly exercise shakti is to gradually burn away all impurities in the physical body, rejuvenating as well as purifying the body. Shakti is "psychic energy" capable of uniting with "cosmic energy" to fulfill the potential of a person and give those kinds of experiences typically associated with "Enlightenment." In the human organism, Kundalini is the "supreme force."

There is a Tradition which says that there once existed an elaborate system of sexual mysticism and magic originating with Sekhmet and which later was lost, perhaps taken away by Her. Important for this system were both the Kundalini energy and those centers of psychic energy known in India as *chakras*. The fact that the ancient Egyptians knew about Chakras and Kundalini Shakti has been asserted by two of the world's leading authorities on myth, magic and religion. Joseph Campbell, generally regarded as the world's foremost mythologist, described the evidence for the existence of this knowledge in Egypt in the January 1982 issue of the journal *Parabola* and has also affirmed this in public lectures and conversations with the author. Kenneth Grant, leading authority on magic and head of the *Ordo Templi Orientis*, once personal secretary to Aleister Crowley, has identified the Goddess Sekhmet with Kundalini and discussed the knowledge of the Chakras in Egypt in personal communications to the author. The word *shakti* is itself a Hindu derivation from the name Sekhmet.

In the Sekhmet Work, as in Tantric and other Yoga practices, the main goal of merging Kundalini energy with "cosmic consciousness" is to realize oneself completely—that is, to actualize one's full potentials. In the Way of the Five Bodies of Sekhmet, the "raising" of Kundalini is easier to achieve and not at all so devastating to the gross physical body and the mind (the bodies AUFU and KA) since it is only done by a person who has awakened and integrated the higher subtle bodies. Failure to first awaken and integrate the subtle bodies results in the familiar outcomes of the awakening of Kundalini—terrible suffering and, not infrequently, madness, death, or both. Let the reader consider the case of Gopi Krishna!

Concerning the Goddess Sekhmet, more biographical information will become available from the scrutiny of some of Her Names and "Epithets." Something still should be said here, however, about statues of the Goddess and also about the crucial importance for Egyptian magic and religion of idols and other representations of deities.

No other deity of ancient Egypt is represented by so many large statues as is Sekhmet. Most of the existing large statues of the Goddess were created by order of Amenhotep III (18th Dynasty: 1411-1375 B.C.) and of those, most of the ones surviving are at Karnak. It has been estimated that the number of statues placed there was 572.

Another very great but unknown number of large Sekhmet statues were placed by Amenhotep in and around his temple at Kurneh, on the opposite and western bank of the Nile at Thebes. This site is known today as the Kom el Heitan. Why these monumental statues of the Goddess exist in such unrivaled numbers has never been satisfactorily explained, although it is conjectured that they may have been promised to Sekhmet in Her healing role or to terminate a pestilence.

With respect to magical and religious power, it was not in such monuments that it resided, but rather in statues cared for and worked with in temples and other places of magical working, and the greatest power resided in certain especially sacred small statues (what are sometimes called "cultus images"), fashioned according to strict cosmic laws and intended for the most important rites and other purposes. Such an "essential" statue of a Deity was kept in the innermost chamber of the temple sacred to the God or Goddess represented, and it was carefully guarded and tended by the priests. The "essential statue" was brought out only on special occasions, such as great festivals. It was usually not made of costly materials, but the Deity was believed to be present in an unusually immediate and potent way and, through the statue, carried out most communication with the priests.

Such a statue had the capacity to heal, to overcome enemies, to perform a great many other magical and miraculous feats, but most important of all, to *teach*. The statue sometimes moved—for example, when performing the movement called *Hanu*, a gesture of the head or hand designating some person as having been "seized by the God"—that is, selected for a special role or purpose. A God or Goddess could also be communicated with by means of less powerful statues, which were charged at regular intervals by means of magical-religious rites. All of these magical statues and idols became more powerful the more they were worked with and worshipped.

In considering the statues, it must be clearly understood that idols are experienced not just as representations of a God, but as "Theophanies," as the Living God. The God exists apart from the idol, of course, but it is through the images, the magical statue or other "objective work of art" (when it is that) that the interaction of human with Deity takes place. In addition to those material images, subtler mental (visual) images of the Deity can also be worked with in magical-religious practice. Both the material and mental image may serve as a means of awakening "Cognitive Imagination" so that the Living Goddess may be experienced in the Visionary World. In other words, by means of the practice with objective and mental images, the practitioner may become a Visionary able to penetrate into otherwise hidden spiritual dimensions. Such ability, however, is far from being all that is required of the magician-priest—as the account of The Way of the Five Bodies has made plain.

[1] E.A. Wallis Budge, *The Gods of the Egyptians: Studies in Egyptian Mythology*, Vol. 1, Dover, New York, p. 515.
[2] Gerald Massey, *Ancient Egypt*. Vol. 2, Samuel Weiser, York Beach, ME, 1970, p. 698. This work was first published in 1907.
[3] Massey, *Ancient Egypt*, Vol. 1, Samuel Weiser, York Beach, ME, 1970, p. 250.

NAMES OF THE GODDESS SEKHMET

According to the magical Tradition, there are some four thousand "Names" of the Goddess Sekhmet. These Names, sometimes also referred to as "Epithets," describe various aspects and attributes of the Goddess, are "Titles" accorded Her, refer to events and places connected to Her, or relate to Her in some other way. The "Names" are thus valuable just as biographical materials, but they also have uses of much greater importance. This is true because each of the Names is represented by another Name or Word of Power. These "Words of Power," or HEKAU, have many uses in doing the Work of Sekhmet, including relating to the Goddess and, for example, facilitating the practice of meditation.

Again according to the sacred Tradition, of the four thousand Names of the Goddess Sekhmet, one thousand Names were known only to the Gods, and another one thousand were known only to the Gods and to some other higher nonhuman beings of the kinds known as angels and demons, or eudemons and cacodemons—the highest among good and evil spirits. Of the remaining two thousand Names, one thousand were accessible only to magician-priests of the Goddess, and according to their level of initiation. These were individuals who had made conscious and functional the KHU and/or SÂHU bodies. Of the remaining one thousand Names, five hundred were known only to the magician-priests and to others who were on the Path or Way of the Goddess and, again, those Names which were known were taught in terms of individual development or initiation. And the remaining five hundred Names were "for the people." One Name, out of these four thousand Names, was considered to be the "Highest" and was known only to the Goddess and a few other Gods and Goddesses—including Her Ennead, or The Eight associated Deities—and to the ruling Pharaoh. There was also one other Name, known only to Sekhmet, by means of which the Goddess could "modify Her Being," and even cease to Be. This possibility *Not to Be* distinguishes the Gods and Goddesses of Egypt from Deities of other Pantheons.

Almost all of these Names have now been lost so that only a few hundred have survived in ancient manuscripts. However, all of the two thousand Names accessible to the magician-priests have been preserved in that Cosmic Memory Bank or Hall of Records called *The Pharaonic Line* and to which a few Adepts may still be presumed to have some access.

As mentioned, there are Words of Power (HEKAU) which can be uttered to evoke the Goddess or attributes of the Goddess described or suggested in the various Names and Epithets. Those *Hekau*, which later came to be known in India as *Mantra* and *Shabda*—"Words of Power" and "Sacred Sounds"—were the "Names" spoken of earlier as being known only to the Gods, certain other nonhuman beings, and the magician-priests. They were, in fact, not "words" at all in the conventional sense but sacred sounds accompanied in each case by an image, a posture, gestures, rhythms and vibrations and still other accompaniments, having only a single significance and giving rise to no associations which might dilute the "Word's" power. In addition to *Hekau* for the Names of the Goddess, there were *Hekau* for each of Her Bodies, Her Souls, and for other components of Her Being. And there were not only *Hekau* for the Gods, but every being and thing in existence was *Named* and could be affected through its Name by anyone who had requisite knowledge to enable him/her to utter it with all the necessary accompaniments. *Hekau* thus could affect all of Being—and by *Naming*, most of Being was created, or "In the Beginning was the 'Word,' " as it has been put by the Hebrews. Thus, *Hekau* remains very largely the secret of the Gods, and most Words of Power known to magician-priests are those Names of the Gods which serve the purposes of a particular God or Goddess and a particular Way.

In the Way of the Goddess Sekhmet, those *Hekau* which are made known are provided by the Goddess first of all and by Teachers or magician-priests to pupils or initiates. They are generally given for several purposes in addition to evoking the Goddess in a particular aspect or as a way of evoking in oneself certain qualities or attributes which represent some aspect of the Goddess. Among these other purposes and effects:

Achieving altered states of consciousness most suitable for realizing objectives;

Affecting other persons—for example, healing;

As a way of prayer;

And as a means for personal development.

As with Mantra, Hekau will be effective only if understood fully and executed perfectly. Otherwise, a potential Word of Power can be said ten million times without the slightest result.

Specifically in Sekhmet's Way of the Five Bodies, a different Name is assigned to each of the five bodies as the Work progresses. In other words, in the beginning Names are assigned to the AUFU and KA bodies. Later, as the Work successfully continues and the higher subtle bodies are made conscious and integrated with the other conscious bodies, then they are also *Named*. In addition to this, each individual has one Name given to that person by his/her Teacher which refers to the totality of that person's Being. This is the essential "magical" and "secret" Name of that person and it must be guarded with extreme care. Anyone who knows that *assigned* Name of the person has great power over him/her—power which can be used either constructively or destructively. When the pupil or initiate accepts or allows him- or herself to be "Named," that is an act of great faith in the Teacher or magician-priest. On the other side, the one who Names the pupil knows very well the *severe* karmic penalties involved in misusing the *Naming*.

The Magical Assigned Name can be of great benefit to the person when it is used as a means of self-actualization—used, for example, as a *Mantra* in certain kinds of meditation. A Teacher who gives the Name to a pupil provides a Name that contains and/or represents the entirety of the "Being Essence" of that person. Thus, the Name is much more than the person consciously is or has access to since *it contains both the latent potentials and the entelechy.* As with the Names of the Gods and Goddesses, the Name has various elements.

It has letters, a way it must be spoken, a posture from which it is spoken, often gestures—*mudra*—which accompany the speaking of the Name, a feeling, tone, texture, and sometimes a variety of sensory images in addition to the visual and auditory aspects.

In addition to the Names of Gods and Goddesses, humans and other kinds of Beings, there are also, of course, Words of Power which can be used for various purposes such as, for example, manipulating or controlling natural forces. In some times and in many different countries and cultures, great emphasis is placed on *Hekau* having to do with such creatures as animals, birds, snakes, fishes, and even insects. Even today in Indonesia, for instance, there are persons who have mastered *Hekau* for calling and controlling various animals and serpents and who are willing to demonstrate this capability. In former times, American Indian shamans also are said to have possessed such ability to control animals, birds and other creatures to a very high degree, while the same abilities are attributed to the magician-priests of Hawaii—*Kahunas* and *Alii*. This kind of power, while rare, is still to be found demonstrable by a few initiates in Africa and Central and South America.

Returning now to the publicly known Names and Epithets of the Goddess—which in that form are only latently *Hekau*—some of them do shed considerable additional light on Sekhmet's "personality" as well as the myths, legends and history associated with Her and the varieties of magical-religious practices of Sekhmet's Way. In the following enumeration of one hundred Names and Epithets of the Goddess, ones have been chosen for the purposes just mentioned and also to provide some further acquaintance with the language of the Names and to suggest the scope and diversity of what was Named. The Names have been taken from many sources, including the Sekhmet Tradition and the writings of Egyptologists and others. In the case of the Egyptologists, a special tribute is due Dr. Sigrid-Eike Hoenes, whose dissertation *Untersuchungen zu Wesen und Kult der Göttin Sachmet* was the first full-length study of the Goddess Sekhmet.[4]

---

[4] Published in 1976 by Rudolf Habelt Verlag, Bonn, West Germany.

ONE HUNDRED NAMES AND EPITHETS
OF THE GODDESS SEKHMET

Read now, slowly, the Names of the Goddess, allowing time for each Name to pass through your conscious mind and into your unconscious, there taking root. In this way, you will begin to experience much more fully the powerful Reality that is Sekhmet. And, as you do that, frequently let your eyes rest on the image of Sekhmet on the page containing the Names of Sekhmet. That will further the same purpose as savoring the Names—the Goddess will become active within you, and you will become one born of Sekhmet, the Great Mother. You can begin to experience the trances that will lead you towards The Way of the Five Bodies. Intend to go deeper into trance, into the Mystery, and you will go deeper as you contemplate the Names, as you contemplate the images.

SEKHMET, GREAT
ONE OF MAGIC

MOTHER OF THE
GODS

ONE WHO WAS
BEFORE THE GODS
WERE

LADY OF THE
PLACE OF THE
BEGINNING OF
TIME

BELOVED OF RA,
HER FATHER

BELOVED OF BAST,
HER SISTER

BELOVED OF PTAH,
HER HUSBAND-
BROTHER

AT WHOSE WISH
THE ARTS WERE
BORN

BEAUTIFUL EYE
WHICH GIVETH
LIFE TO THE TWO
LANDS

BEAUTIFUL FACE,
IMAGE MOST
BELOVED BY ART

FLAMING ONE

SOVEREIGN OF RA, HER FATHER

PROTECTRESS OF THE GODS

LADY OF THE SCARLET-COLORED GARMENT

PURE ONE

DESTROYER OF REBELLIONS

EYE OF RA

EYE OF HORUS

PRE-EMINENT ONE IN THE BOAT OF
THE MILLIONS OF YEARS

ROAMER OF DESERTS

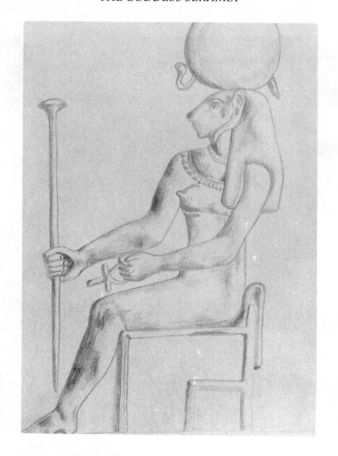

WANDERER IN THE WASTES

SELF-CONTAINED

ONLY ONE

AWAKENER

LADY OF ENCHANTMENTS

OPENER OF WAYS

LADY OF TRANSFORMATIONS

LADY OF THE MANY FACES

ENRAPTURING ONE

GIVER OF ECSTASIES

SATISFIER OF
DESIRES

INSPIRER OF
MALES

VICTORIOUS ONE
IN BATTLES

OVERCOMER OF ALL
ENEMIES

RULER OF THE
DESERT

RULER OF
SERPENTS AND OF
DRAGONS

RULER OF LIONS

COMPLETE ONE

SUBLIME ONE

ENLIGHTENER

EMPOWERER

SPARKLING ONE

GREAT ONE OF HEKAU

LADY OF THE MAGIC
LAMP

MOTHER OF THE DEAD

LADY OF THE BLOODBATH

DESTROYER BY PLAGUES

GREAT ONE OF HEALING

DESTROYER BY FIRE

LADY OF THE WATERS OF LIFE

MISTRESS AND LADY OF THE TOMB

GREAT ONE IN THE PLACES
OF JUDGMENT AND EXECUTION

GUIDE AND PROTECTRESS FROM THE
PERILS OF THE UNDERWORLD

GREAT ONE OF THE PLACE OF
APPEARANCES IN SILENCE

LADY OF THE WAY OF THE FIVE BODIES

UNRIVALED AND INVINCIBLE ONE

RULER OF THE CHAMBER OF FLAMES

THE SOURCE

SHE WHOSE OPPORTUNITY ESCAPETH HER NOT

WINGED ONE

POWERFUL OF HEART

THE AWARE

THE GLEAMING ONE

SEKHMET, WHO
REDUCETH TO
SILENCE

SEKHMET, WHO
ROUSETH THE
PEOPLE

LADY OF
JUBILATION

ADORABLE ONE

SHINING OF
COUNTENANCE

MOTHER OF
IMAGES

INCOMPARABLE
ONE

LADY OF INTOXICA-
TIONS

MIGHTIER THAN THE
GODS

MOST BEAUTIFUL

MOST STRONG

GREAT ONE OF LAWS

PROTECTRESS OF THE DIVINE ORDER

THE ONE WHO HOLDS BACK DARKNESS

THE BEAUTIFUL LIGHT

WARRIOR GODDESS

GODDESS OF LOVE

GREAT ONE IN HEAVEN

GREAT SERPENT ON THE HEAD OF HER FATHER

GREAT ONE OF THE INCENSE OF THE ENNEAD

GREAT LADY OF THE HOUSE OF LIFE

QUEEN OF THE VENERABLE ONES

LADY OF THE HOUSE OF BOOKS

DEVOURING ONE

SEKHMET OF THE KNIVES

BURNER OF EVILDOERS

ONE BEFORE WHOM EVIL TREMBLES

TERRIBLE ONE

LADY OF ALL POWERS

ETERNAL AS HER FATHER

LADY OF THE MANIFOLD ADORNMENTS

MOST BEAUTIFUL AMONG THE GODS

BOUNTIFUL ONE

SEKHMET, WHO GIVES JOYS

UNWAVERING LOYAL ONE

BELOVED TEACHER

BELOVED SEKHMET

INTERNALIZING THE IMAGE
OF THE
GODDESS SEKHMET

The experience you now are invited to participate in is intended to help you internalize the image of the Goddess Sekhmet. When you have done this, you will be better able to meditate on that image, go into trance, and encourage within yourself access to the Goddess and Her Teachings. When the image is well internalized, then the Work can be done independently of any object such as a statue or a photograph. However, it will always be useful to have access to such objects, especially ones created for the purpose of gaining access to Sekhmet—and created by persons having knowledge of how to fashion such images.

To some extent, the process of internalizing the image of the Goddess has begun within you already. The photographs in this book and the words you have read in it already have given Her very powerful image a place not only in your conscious mind, but also in your unconscious. It may be that already in your spiritual depths you have made a very strong response to Sekhmet, that your soul resonates to Her image.

In order to *intensify and deepen your experience of the Goddess*, in order that you may *know in a more immediate and profound way the Being of Sekhmet, the Powers and the Essence of Sekhmet*, select now one of the photographs of Her as represented by the statue on the cover of this book. Look with care at the various pictures of *that statue*, and select the one that affects you most strongly. Select that photograph, but then do look again for a while at some of the other photographs of the same statue, making certain that you know very well the entirety of the statue, including the lower body and the throne upon which Sekhmet is seated. The image you choose to Work with might be one that shows Sekhmet's upper body only, but you must then have in mind the totality of the statue as you do your Work with the picture you have selected as most powerful for you. Later you may Work with any of the images of the Goddess, but it is imperative that you begin with an image of the *essential statue,* that image the Goddess Sekhmet has *indwelled.*

The purpose of the instructions hereafter provided will be to enable you to maintain without difficulty your focus of attention on the image of the Goddess for a period of time considerably longer than you would probably be able to maintain that focus otherwise. This is the case, unless you have already gained proficiency in such disciplines as concentration and meditation. Because you must focus upon Sekhmet's image, the following Way of internalizing Her image will have to be read to you, or you must devise another way of overcoming the problem. The Work to *internalize the image* should be done with the highest level of concentration, the highest quality of consciousness you are able to bring to the Work.

Look now very carefully at the image before you. Observe first of all the solar or sun disc on Her head. In the center of that disc observe the standing form of the cobra known as the uraeus serpent, and note the inlaid golden eyes of the lioness-headed Sekhmet. If you focus on the solar disc and the cobra, or if you focus on the eyes of Sekhmet, you should find it already very easy to begin to go into trance. And then to go deeper as you continue to focus on the disc and the cobra, or on the eyes, or perhaps the whole head and the mane that surrounds it. Silently focus now on whatever seems the more powerfully to lay hold on your consciousness so that you can experience your consciousness altering, the focus of consciousness narrowing as you go deeper.

As you look at Her closely and as the world around you increasingly recedes from your awareness, notice whether that figure begins to become three-dimensional. Observe whether it is not now already standing out from the background in a way it did not when you first looked at it. Observe if there is not coming into this image for you an increasing sense or awareness that there is life in the image. As you continue to concentrate, remark if this quality of being alive does not become more pronounced.

For well over three thousand years, this particular statue of Sekhmet has existed. Human eyes have rested upon it since the times when in Ancient Egypt the statue had its place in the great Temple of Karnak, there to be venerated and worked with by the magician-priests. Look at Her. She is the Great Mother. The Pharaoh Rameses II claimed her as being literally the Mother of his souls and higher bodies.

Observe for a moment Her hands and how the thumbs rest on the fingers of Her hands. In this position as She sits now, and as you closely observe Her hands, know that the thumbs were used to beam energy for healing and for transferring some of the energy of the Goddess into human bodies. Look at Her closely and imagine Her turning so that She faces you directly and the thumbs send that energy into various parts of your body. You might feel Her beaming it into your belly or into your heart, your throat, your third eye, your brain, and when She does this there is often to be seen a smoky energy surrounding Her or swirling around Her. Look at Her very, very closely and note whether you feel in your body, or can see, that energy She emanates.

According to Tradition, such a statue as this one, when indwelled by the Goddess, could see and hear and speak, and other parts of its body could move also. Imagine Her now arising from Her throne and standing with Her right arm extended, then lowering the arm so that when the arm lowers there has appeared in Her hand a golden ankh.

Look at Her before you and at the same time imagine Her roaming the desert in Her lion's body. She is a complete lioness now, but enormous and numinous—that lioness form that provided the model for every lioness who came after it. Wandering the desert under the scorching sun and wandering at night beneath the moon.

Looking at Her, think of the festivals and revelries staged to celebrate Her actions and Her Being, and let your eyes just roam for a while over Her image while you remember that She is one of the most ancient of all Deities known to humans. She is the Lady of the Place of the Beginning of Time, the One Who Was Before the Gods Were, the Great One of Magic. Look at Her now as if you were looking out of the eyes of an Ancient Egyptian, a priest or priestess or magician of Sekhmet, or a magician-priest or magician-priestess intent upon learning from Her the mysteries which She represents.

Look at Her and go deeper and deeper and deeper. Let Her penetrate ever more deeply into your unconscious mind, and know that by doing that you can come to know Her and learn much about Her magic, Her religion, who She IS. Then close your eyes for a moment and continue to see Her as vividly as possible so that in that way She becomes one with you even more completely.

When you have opened your eyes, look at the picture again. See if the quality of life in the image is not now even stronger, and note if even now it remains very easy to continue to focus on that image. You may find that you have very little inclination now to focus on anything else, that everything around you in this moment has much less interest, that the image of Sekhmet is far more present for you and far more real than anything else in your surroundings. Does Her image seem larger than before? More dimensional and even still more alive? You understand now something more about the magic of Sekhmet, Her mystery and Her power.

Continue now to look at that image for as long as you wish, and then terminate this meditation and internalization of the Goddess Sekhmet when you choose to do so. Having come this far, you surely will return again.

SA SEKHEM SÂHU

SA SEKHEM SÂHU is the first mantra to be practiced by all initiates on The Way of the Five Bodies. It is practiced in addition to a meditation in which there is simply a combined concentration on the Name SEKHMET and on an image of the Goddess such as the ones provided for that purpose in this book.

The SA is the "Breath of Life" already discussed.

The SÂHU is the realized human being—the one who has awakened and integrated the five bodies.

SEKHEM means "Power" or "Might" and, in the case of the SÂHU, is also the Force which animates the SÂHU's body and provides it with special powers not possessed by the less subtle bodies. The SÂHU body also requires the SA, or Breath of Life, but SEKHEM provides a "something additional" required for a body of such subtlety. SEKHEM is present, too, in the "bodies" of the Gods. As a magical energy, SEKHEM is also accessible to the KHU body, but is not a permanent part of it.

The meditation mantra—SA SEKHEM SÂHU—should be performed by all persons on the Goddess Sekhmet's Way, including those who do not yet have experiential knowledge of the effects of these Power Words, with the understanding that the Words signify:

THE BREATH OF LIFE
THE SACRED MIGHT
THE REALIZED HUMAN

When the mantra is taught, the pronunciation is also taught, of course, so that the Words of Power are, at the same time, Sacred Sounds. It is beneficial to do this mantra, however, even without the exact pronunciation being known. The Goddess Sekhmet will respond to the intention of the meditator. The SA and SÂHU may be approximated by an "ah" sound for the SA, and adding a "hoo" sound for the SÂHU. In pronouncing SEKHEM, the first syllable is an "eh" sound, the second as in the English word "hem." In pronouncing the words, the accent is on the second syllable. When meditating on the Name SEKHMET, the pronunciation of the vowels is similar to that in the case of the Word SEKHEM. However, the meditator is encouraged to otherwise experiment with many ways of pronouncing SEKHMET, observing the effects.

These Words of Power are always to some extent evocative of the Goddess and become more so when accompanied by a mental image of Sekhmet or when meditating on a picture or statue of the Goddess. The Words should be repeated many times, without mind-wandering or other distraction, but with sufficient self-observation to become aware of altered bodily, mental, emotional or other states. The meditation can be done as often as desired, but at least several times each day.

FIFTH WAY PSYCHOSPIRITUAL EXERCISES

Preliminary Remarks

The *Psychospiritual Exercises* to be presented in this segment of the book are offered as examples of some of the Work of a Fifth Way Mystery School, or a School following the Goddess Sekhmet's Way of the Five Bodies. These exercises can also be done as primarily psychological ones and also as a means of improving the health and functioning of the brain and nervous system. Then, they benefit health and functioning generally and can be used quite specifically for many kinds of self-healing. Depending upon the teaching intention, these exercises would be combined with other appropriate ones, furthering the respective aims.

In either case, such work would typically be preceded by exercises of kinds referred to as *psychophysical*. Such exercises, known as Psychophysical Method, or sometimes as Masters Technique, might be thought of as the Fifth Way's *Hatha Yoga*. Those exercises have as their primary aim the reorganization of the musculoskeletal system: sensory and neural re-education; the bringing about of coincidence between the physical body and the body image; movement disinhibition and training in the applications of body mechanics; and the establishing of a generally much more effective use of the body, including many basic understandings of, and ability to make use of, mind-body interrelationships.

Such basic work has been described by the author of this vol-

77

ume in numerous publications, including the books *Listening to the Body* (with Jean Houston); *Psychophysical Method Exercises* (Vols. I-VI); and the forthcoming *The Masters Technique*, to be published in the near future. Many teachers of the technique have been trained by the author, and there is an Association for the Masters Psychophysical Method. To the extent that those teachers make use of exercises the same as or similar to the ones contained in this book, use of the exercises occurs within a *psychological* and *psychophysical* but not a *psychospiritual* context. Only in a Fifth Way Esoteric School, and accompanied by much other and different Work, do the exercises serve those purposes which make them truly psychospiritual.

In the case of the training of the magician-priest or -priestess on The Way of the Five Bodies, then, there would be a thorough grounding in psychological and psychophysical exercises which would precede psychospiritual work. Nonetheless, it is possible to practice the following exercises and gain considerable benefits from them while also gaining many glimpses into the kinds of Work that must be done in a School.

The exercises as taught in the School aim eventually, of course, at the awakening and integration of the subtle bodies and at making accessible many potentials which exist in almost all human beings as latencies only. At the same time, however, and to achieve such purposes, it is absolutely essential to re-educate the nervous system and do the other re-educational and organizational work on the body mentioned earlier. The ordinary human being has so little knowledge, much less understanding, of his/her own organism that even the barest rudiments of such knowledge often are astonishing when experienced. The exercises here provided will begin to fill in that terribly crippling void left by what passes in the schools of today as "education." (In ancient times, as many still know, such *real* education concerning the use of the self—body, mind and spirit—was considered to be the absolutely essential preparation for all other education. But even that *goal* has been lost.)

An important part of the Work of a Fifth Way School is to enable a student to move in a self-regulated way along an ever-increasing continuum of states of consciousness accessible to the student. In possibly more familiar language, this would be stated as the learned ability of the student to recognize and self-regulate depth of trance. The student would learn by the experience of many different levels that "point" on the continuum of states of consciousness which should be chosen as optimal for whatever it is that he/she wishes to do. This includes the self-regulation of the body, including bodily functions usually thought of as *involuntary*—such as brain wave production, blood flow, heart rate, and so on. Even in the absence of the ability to self-select states of consciousness, however, it is possible to use very simple—yet typically unknown—methods to bring about many significant changes in bodily organization and functioning. In some of the brief opening exercises, for example, it will be demonstrated that it is possible to markedly alter the musculoskeletal organization and the body image (body as sensed or experienced) simply by using words, or just visual images, or tactile and kinesthetic images, separately or in combination. Once the person has learned to elicit responses from the body by those means and at those levels, then it becomes possible to influence various organs and processes which are not usually thought of as able to be affected by means of conscious controls. Various exercises will establish the possibility of using consciousness focused in a variety of ways to effect changes physical, mental and emotional. It will also be demonstrated, for example, that *by means of orchestrated sensing, a person can accumulate Being, so that Presence is enhanced in a way that is readily recognizable by others.*

Beyond the use of words and sensory images to alter body, mind and emotions lies the work with "imagined bodies" or "image bodies." Within the experience of the untutored individual, the only analogous experience is that of one's body as experienced in dreams. It is possible to create image bodies in which any changes will be mirrored by the physical body (as, in fact, often happens in the case of the dream body—as in sexual dreams). This could obviously be of great therapeutic benefit should the physical body be so immobilized that the desired changes in it could be achieved only by means of such mirroring of the changes effected in the image body. Other image bodies are created which do *not* create such mirroring by the gross physical body, but may bring about changes in any of the subtle bodies. Work with image bodies, then, becomes an important means whereby the subtle bodies can be awakened and differentiated. The following psychospiritual exercises also offer techniques which enable a person to identify consciousness with his/her *whole* body and not just with a part of it, as is the norm in a great many cultures. (Examples of such "localization" will be given in the exercise titled "Examining the 'I'.") Preliminary work will be done to prepare the student for penetrating into other realities and for the awakening of those *psychospiritual senses* by means of which such realities can be apprehended in ways inaccessible to the physical body's sensory mechanisms.

By means of movement, sensing and directing focus of consciousness, the body can be used to achieve altered states of consciousness important for the work. The available range of states of consciousness *must* be very greatly increased in order for the work with the KHU and SÂHU bodies even to begin to be done, and a considerable range of altered states must become accessible even well in advance of that more difficult Work.

There is another quite important point that should be mentioned. These exercises in themselves, and even in the absence of a Teacher, *are an initiatory process.* Just to do them—and to do them well—draws the doer into the context of Fifth Way Work. It thus also brings such a person closer to a School, to the Goddess Sekhmet, or both. It then helps to bring about that situation—known in all esoteric Work—where "When the pupil is ready, the Teacher will appear." For everyone, even if he/she does not aspire to follow a particular Way, the doing of the exercises will increase the awareness of, and ability to use, more latent human potentials. Whatever the individual goals, those who do the exercises well, and who have read this book with sufficient mindfulness and understanding, will certainly move beyond that level of personal Being as it was before the Work was done.

PRACTICAL NOTES

The following very practical instructions also require attention:

In the case of most of the exercises, it is difficult to do them just by reading from the book. It is much better to work with another person, or in a small group, one person reading the exercises while the other(s) perform(s) them. It is also, of course, quite possible to tape the exercises for oneself and then listen to the tape. In either case, timing is essential so that the work can be done in a manner that emphasizes quality of consciousness and allows for the optimal number of repetitions of movements—usually about 25 repetitions of a movement.

The work should be done in a comfortable, distraction-free environment. Clothing should not impede movement. Nothing should be done that is physically difficult or creates feelings of strain or pain. When any kind of exercise is unpleasant, it naturally evokes resistance, creates internal conflicts and otherwise erodes motivation and interferes with the attaining of optimal results. Should physical movements become tiring, then continue the movements by means of sensory images, imaging as clearly as possible just what the movements would feel like if physically done. Then, when rested, resume doing them in the more objective way. It cannot be emphasized too strongly that the results obtained will most of all depend upon the quality of consciousness brought to the exercises. Think of the movements as sacred ones, and keep in mind what has been said of such movements in so many of the ancient esoteric Schools throughout the world: "Always move as if praying with your body." In fact, it was a goal of such Schools that this eventually be applied to *all* of a person's movements, not just those thought of as "exercises." *Ideally, all movement is meditation; all of life, Spiritual Exercise.*

TALKING TO THE BODY

This exercise and all subsequent ones will be written with the intention that the words are to be spoken. In terms of the senses, these words are for the ears, not for the eyes.

Before beginning, and to recapitulate briefly, the human body will respond in both minor and far-reaching ways to verbal suggestions or instructions (commands) and to various sensory images or combinations of such images. In some cases, this response will occur provided only that consciousness remains focused on the part(s) or function(s) being addressed. In other cases, changes may be more profound, depending upon how profoundly consciousness is altered or upon how appropriate is the level of consciousness to the change being sought.

To do the exercise, you will need a straight-backed chair without any cushioning. Just be seated with your palms down on top of your legs; let the hands rest lightly on the legs, and also let the soles of your feet rest lightly on the floor. Arrange the whole of your body so that you can easily maintain the way in which you are seated. Then close your eyes.

Throughout this exercise, you will be focusing and working on the right side of your body. But first, compare the two sides as they now are. Do you sit equally on the two sides? Do the parts on each side feel to you to be the same? Are they about equally clear in your body image? Compare, for example, how you sense the right eye and the left one; the right hand and the left one; the right leg and the left leg. Does your head face to the front, as it should in the beginning? And is the same true of your eyes?

Remember what it was you observed.

Remember that you are only to talk to your body. Do not try to imagine what a movement looks like or any of the sensations of movement involved in what will be suggested. Also remember that you are addressing only the right side of your body.

Now, speaking just to the whole of your right foot, repeat half a dozen times, "Toes loosening and lengthening."[5] "Toes loosening and lengthening." "Toes extending and getting longer." Continue to address your right foot.

Always, when doing these exercises, endeavor to notice as completely as possible whether your body is responding, and if it is, just how it is responding. Whether it responds is unimportant, but self-observe very closely and make certain that you do not hold your breath.

Again addressing your right foot: "The right foot loosening and lengthening." "The whole right foot loosening and lengthening." "The right foot lengthening and also making better contact with the floor." (Remember to repeat each instruction a number of times.)

And now: "Lower right leg is lengthening." "My lower right leg getting longer." Continue repeating those words and observe whatever you experience.

"Right knee releasing." "Right knee releasing."

"Upper right leg getting longer." "Right upper leg loosening and lengthening." "My entire right leg, my right foot and toes getting longer."

Direct your attention for a moment to your eyes. In what direction are they looking? Is your head still facing forward, or has it turned or cocked somewhat to the right? If your head and eyes are not facing forward, then arrange yourself so that they do that. And then continue talking to your right side.

"Right side of the pelvis releasing." "Right hip joint releasing." "Right buttock sinking lower." "The whole right side of my pelvis releasing."

"Right side of my upper body getting longer." "My rib cage releasing on the right side." (Always allow time to repeat the instructions, in this exercise at least a half dozen times.) "Breathing more freely on the right side." "Breathing involving more and more of my body on the right side."

Now observe your breathing. Notice if, in fact, you now do breathe better and use more of your body on the right side. By now this probably will be the case if your breathing was symmetrical between the two sides, or almost so, at the beginning.

"Fingers of the right hand loosening and lengthening." "Fingers of the right hand loosening and lengthening." "Whole right hand lengthening and lying flatter on your leg as it loosens and lengthens."

"Right wrist releasing." "Right forearm loosening and lengthening." "Right forearm loosening and lengthening."

"Now the right elbow releasing." "Right upper arm lengthening and loosening." "The right upper arm loosening and lengthening."

"Right shoulder releasing." "Right shoulder releasing." "The neck getting longer on the right side." "The neck loosening and lengthening."

Observe once again the position of your head and where your eyes are looking. Observe again your breathing, comparing the two sides. Also note where your tongue is lying.

Notice if you sit more to the right side than before, so that your body has tilted somewhat. Compare the contact with the chair of your right buttock and your left. Compare the way you sense your body on the right side with the way you sense your body on the left side. Also compare different parts: the right eye with the left eye; the right side of the mouth with the left side; the right hand with the left; the right foot with the left. Do you notice a difference in the clarity with which you are sensing those different sides and parts? Does your right foot make a different contact with the floor than your left foot? Does your right hand make a different contact with your leg than does your left hand? Does it sense better what it is touching? Does what your right hand touches feel more alive? What other differences can you discover? And self-observe now with your eyes open.

Slide your hands down across your knees and down onto your lower legs. Compare what you touch and also compare how far you reach. It may well be the case that the right arm reaches farther than the left one. Actually, the right arm may now be longer.

Remember that, until just now, you have not been making any movements. You have only been addressing your body and observing its responses. Yet, unless you have done such work before, the differences between the two sides of your body are probably greater than any you ever have experienced in your lifetime.

Your awareness of the two sides—the differences between them—is surely more complete than it ever has been before.

It has taken many complicated internal changes to create the effects which you have just experienced. These should make evident to you that you might also be able to change almost any other parts or functions of your body just by talking.

What you accomplished here has occurred with a body that has not been trained to respond to your instructions or suggestions. Consider then what you might be able to achieve with frequent and regular practice over a period of months or longer.

Once more now, close your eyes. Self-observe and note whether you already again sit somewhat more equally, or even quite symmetrically. To what extent has the whole of your body returned to its originally more symmetrical organization?

In the next several lessons, we will explore other ways of altering sensing and body image, organization and movement, and of effecting other important changes by predominantly mental means.

---

[5] When teaching another person, you may want to say "your toes." If you are making a tape, then you may want to say "my toes." Or you can always just say "the toes" or "the hand" or "the right foot," and so on. In this respect, but in few others, feel free to modify the text.

VISUALIZING
BODY MOVEMENT

The human body can be deliberately and rather precisely altered in many ways by means of words, by means of sensory images, or by combinations of words and images. In this exercise, *visual* images will be used to alter the *left side* of the body.

While words will be used to provide you with particular visual images, your response should differ very little, if at all, from the response you would make were you to provide your own visual images apart from any words.

A human body will respond to visual images, and it will also respond in various ways desired to tactile (touch) images and to kinesthetic images (images of movement sensations). The other sensory imageries—taste, sound, smell, pleasure sensations not readily assignable to the other sense modes—also can be used to elicit predictable responses in ways not experienced in everyday life.

Before beginning this exercise, it should be noted that in this book a distinction is made between "imaging" and "imagining" sensory experiences. To "imagine," according to this distinction, is to know approximately what something would be like without having a strong and immediate sensory knowledge akin to the experience of the physical senses. To "image," on the other hand, is to have as strong a sensory response as possible, but to a stimulus existing in the mind rather than, as is usual, in the external world. The sensory

87

response in "imaging" is to a *subjective* rather than to an objective reality.

The distinction is of primary importance since the response of
the brain, and then other parts of the body, differs greatly between
"imagined" and "imaged" experiences. When the sensory images
are strong enough, then the brain is "deceived" and the body responds to the subjective reality exactly, or almost exactly, as it
would to an objective reality. It is the *experienced intensity of the sensing* that distinguishes an imagined act or event from an imaged one.

In the case of an exercise such as this one, in practice it is perhaps impossible to achieve a true purity of sensory imaging—that
is, to image *just one sense mode* when trying to *just visually* image
movement. That is true in part because in response to the image the
body organizes itself to some extent to actually execute whatever is
being imaged. And if one is sensitive enough, then that organization
will be sensed.

For example, if you try to image making a fist with your left
hand, and especially if trying to image making a very tight fist, and
are sufficiently sensitive, then you will feel that the muscles are
moving in at least a slight way to make the fist that the mind is imaging. Thus, a kinesthetic or movement image is likely to "contami-
nate" the intended purity of the visual image.

Nevertheless, you should try very hard now to be pure, but not
to the extent of holding your breath. We want to work *only* with
visual images for a while, to the extent that it is possible, and we will
be working just with the left side.

Arrange yourself so that you are comfortably seated in a chair,
preferably with one hand palm down on the thigh of each leg, and
just above the knee. The fingers can be on the knees. Let both feet
stand side by side at a comfortable distance apart, and with the bottoms of both feet resting lightly on the floor.

Now visualize the left side of your body with your eyes closed.
Try to picture your left foot and your left lower leg and knee. Picture
your left upper leg, your hip joint, and the left side of your pelvis.
Picture the whole left side of your lower body.

Picture the left fingers and hand and the left wrist. Picture the
left forearm and the elbow. Picture the left upper arm and shoulder.
Picture the whole upper part of your body from the pelvis to the
shoulder on the left side.

Be certain that you include your breathing, and notice whether already your breathing has been affected.

And visualize, too, the left side of your neck, and your face, and your head. Note as you do this whether the eyes look left and if the head has unconsciously been moved left, and perhaps the tongue also.

Then try to visualize the entire left side of your body. Determine if you can visualize yourself as having only a left side, the right side having vanished or become invisible so that it is barely sensed at all.

Now imagine picking up your hand, just slowly raising it off your leg and bending your elbow, so that you imagine the hand approaching your shoulder. If the hand wants to really rise, and does so involuntarily, you can allow it to do that. But have a *visual* image only of bringing the left hand towards the left shoulder and then back down to the left knee. The hand moves up to the shoulder and then back to the knee. Just have a *visual* image.

Then imagine extending the arm out in front of you at shoulder height. Then have a visual image of lowering and raising it, lowering and raising it, but only up to shoulder height.

Next, when you are visually lifting your extended arm, let it go all the way up overhead. Then, keeping it extended, bring it down. Keep on imaging, raising it and lowering it while breathing freely.

When it is above your head, make some circles with it, circling with your hand.

Now picture extending your left arm out to the side at shoulder height, and make some more circles with the arm and the hand. Circle in one direction and then the other. Then let that image of an arm and hand down so that the hand rests on your knee. Image moving the hand so that it rests on the upper part of your thigh and in your lap. Image picking up the left foot and leg and putting it down again. Pick the imaged foot and leg up off the floor and put them down again.

Now image extending the left leg so that you lock the knee and the leg points away from you. The bottom of the foot points out in front of you. Bring the leg down to the floor and extend it again, and keep doing that.

Let the foot rest on the floor.

Then imagine picking it up and making circles with the knee. Pick it up high enough so that the foot is dangling, and you make circles with your knee.

Then reverse the direction of the circling.

Now put it down so your left foot rests on the floor, and image simultaneously extending out in front of you both your left leg and your left arm. The leg is about at the height of the hip joint. The arm is about at the height of the shoulder joint. Then simultaneously picture bending the knee and bending the elbow. Then straighten the leg and arm; and then bend them again. Just keep on doing that.

Then put the hand and the foot back down, and once again try to observe the entire left side of your body as a visual image.

Now just sense that body. Compare the left side with the right. Do you sit more to the left? Do you look to the left? Which side is clearer?

You have previously done the exercise "Talking to the Body." Were the changes greater with the words in that exercise or the visual images in this one?

To what extent could you visually image the movements apart from any kinesthetic images—that is, sensations of movement?

Sense once more how you sit and where you look. Then get up and stretch so that you feel wide awake as well as relaxed.

IMAGES OF MOVEMENT
AND OF TOUCH

Psychological and psychospiritual exercises, especially when done by novices, much more often utilize movement (kinesthetic) and touch (tactile) images than other sensory images or verbal instructions. It is easier to change the body with kinesthetic and tactile images, and yet the beginner will almost always have a much greater difficulty executing such images.

For example, almost anyone can *visually* imagine or image flexing and extending an arm from the elbow. But ask a person to *kinesthetically* image even so familiar a movement, and he/she is likely to be unable to do it without first making the movement objectively in order to determine what sensations accompany it. This illustrates just how fundamentally estranged we are from our bodies. It is necessary to regain knowledge of what sensations accompany what movements before our behavior can even begin to be described as truly conscious.

Because of the inability of almost all contemporary people to sense with accuracy what they are doing or to remember what sensations accompany what movements, in this exercise one or two objective movements will be made first, and then with the sensations still within memory, the remaining movements will be done with kinesthetic and sometimes tactile images.

(It might be added that kinesthetic images are the most impor-

91

tant of all the sensory images for the purpose of bringing about most changes in the body. Kinesthetic images can be used most predictably to bring about changes in the brain and, thereby, in other sensing, thinking and feeling functions. Along with visual images, the kinesthetic ones are also the ones most made use of in achieving the awakening and use of the Five Bodies.)

Again, as in the two previous ones, this exercise can be done while seated in a straight-backed chair without any cushion on the seat. Arrange the body comfortably with, once again, the palms of the hands resting on the upper legs or legs and knees. Compare the two sides for symmetry and for any differences in organization of the body between the two sides or clarity in the body image of the two sides or parts of the two sides.

The soles of your feet should be resting on the floor. Sense (without looking) the distance between your feet and whether your lower legs are approximately vertical, and then confirm or not by looking at what you sensed. Then, without moving, *imagine* raising the heel of your right foot as high off the floor as possible while leaving the ball of the right foot on the floor. What parts of your body must move for you to do that?

Now, physically raise the heel of your right foot as high off the floor as you can while leaving the ball and the toes of the foot on the floor. If you must move the foot closer or farther away from your chair to achieve an optimal raising of the heel, then do that, but do not position the foot so that the heel cannot easily return to the floor. You must be able to lightly and quickly rap with your right heel on the floor.

How well were you able to imagine raising and lowering your right heel? Did you imagine correctly the sensations and the movements of the foot, the ankle, the hip joint, the lower and upper legs? Did you imagine, if your hand was resting on your knee, how the hand would rise with the heel and how that would produce movement in the elbow, and probably also in the upper arm, the right shoulder and in segments of the upper back on your right side? If you now objectively do this movement, you may also note that your body shifts a little to the right, that your eyes look right, your head may turn a little, and even the pattern of the breathing and position of the tongue in your mouth may alter with that movement. So what does this say about your kinesthetic imaging and capacity, and the need for its education and re-education?

For the remainder of this exercise, you will objectively do one or two movements as directed, closely observing those movements, and then repeat them as kinesthetic (and sometimes also tactile) images. Now, bending your right hand from the wrist, remove it a little from the right knee, and then rap a little on the right knee. Do it several times in order to feel the movement in your hand and wrist (and any other movement) and the sensations created in the hand and knee by their contact. Be aware also of the sound of your rap. Now carefully image what you have just physically done. You will be allowed time to image about 15 repetitions of each movement.

Stop. Now several times slide the palm of your right hand down your right leg about halfway to your ankle, and then bring it back up about halfway to your hip joint. Note all the movements you make to do that, probably including bending from your middle, and the touch sensations in the hand and leg and elsewhere. Having done that several times physically, stop and do it with images.

Stop. Taking it out to the side, raise your right arm to shoulder height and then overhead, then bring it back to its starting place with your hand resting on your knee. Do that twice physically, and then do it 15 times with images. Make sure that you do not hold your breath when imaging.

Stop. Place your right fingers on your right shoulder and make circles with the elbow, rotating your right shoulder forward. Sense clearly what you do, and then do it just with images. After 15 such imaged movements, let your right hand come back to rest on your right knee. However, *image* that your right fingers are still on your right shoulder and image making 15 more circles with your elbow, rotating with your shoulder forward. Then image 15 movements, rotating the shoulder back (that is, in just the opposite direction). Then merge the *imaged* hand and arm with the the the one resting on your right leg.

Stop. Keeping your right foot flat on the floor, make circles clockwise with the bottom of your foot, the bent leg rotating from your knee. Then 15 times image doing it, experiencing all sensations vividly. Then image 15 identical movements, except that the circles made by the foot move counterclockwise.

Stop. Scan your body a moment, and especially compare your right side with your left. Try scanning with your eyes open, and then try scanning with your eyes closed. Does that make a difference? Does it make a difference if you focus on specific parts—for example, if you focus on comparing the right foot to the left, the right hand to the left, the right shoulder to the left, the two sides of your face? Is your sitting the same or different on the two sides? Has your awareness of your breathing been affected?

Without first physically moving, try to image rapping with the ball of your right foot on the floor, leaving the right heel on the floor. Where should you place your foot in order to make that rapping optimal, both in terms of ease and also extent of the movement? Try to find that by means of imaging only, and then image the rapping from that position. Now physically rap with the ball of your right foot and notice whether the sensations are as you imagined them. Also, did you identify correctly how the foot and the leg should be positioned? Does it seem to you from this brief last sequence that your ability to kinesthetically image has improved at least slightly?

Twice, pick your whole right foot up and set it down. Then do it 15 times kinesthetically, with a tactile and auditory awareness of your foot making contact with the floor.

Stop. Physically extend your right arm in front of you and reach out as far as you can with the right arm. Then bring it back again, the arm remaining extended out in front of you. Reach out with the arm, and then draw it back, so that the movement is mainly in the right upper back and shoulder. Leaving the arm in front of you, image the movement ten times. Physically, put the hand back onto your right knee, but image the right arm extended out in front of you, and do the movement another 15 times, reaching out and then drawing the arm back. Physically do it two or three more times, and notice whether the movement is the same or different. Then just rest with the hand once again on your leg or on your leg and knee.

Once more compare the two sides. Then stand and walk around, making further comparisons. Compare the movements of the shoulders and arms, the leg movements, and the contact each foot makes with the floor. Try to make other comparisons. What have you achieved by means of this mainly kinesthetic imaging? With practice, even those few physical movements no longer will be needed and considerably greater changes may be brought about just by means of the images.

FREEDOM
THROUGH AWARENESS:
A PRACTICAL
DEMONSTRATION

The following exercise demonstrates in a practical way the importance of awareness for freedom. The power of focused awareness will be used to alter the self-perception, the organization, and the functioning of the body, making it more free.

A considerable number of movements will be performed, and each movement should be repeated about 25 times. To the extent possible, the movements will be simultaneous and identical for both sides of the body. Also as far as possible, awareness will be the only variable with which we work. This means *that while the right and left sides of the body execute identical movements, awareness will be focused on one side only.*

Now, before beginning, it is important to carefully observe your self-perceptions, your musculoskeletal organization, and your functioning as they are at present.

To begin with, lie on your back with your hands at your sides, palms down, and scan your body. Compare your awareness of the parts of your body. Compare the right foot with the left, the right shoulder with the left, and so on.

Note how your body lies, and compare the two sides. Compare the contact with the floor. Flex and extend the various joints, continuing to make comparisons. Note how you breathe through your two nostrils, comparing, and whatever else you sense.

Close your eyes for a moment. Leave the right one closed and open the left, noticing how clearly you see the ceiling above you and your perception of the light in the room. Now open both eyes for a moment. Then close the left eye, open the right, and again note the clarity and light. Compare what you saw with each eye.

Rap with both hands on the floor and listen. Be sure the rapping is equal, and try to detect if you hear the rapping equally. In any other ways you can think of, compare the two sides of your body. Then lie quietly with your palms down at your sides. In a moment we will begin the experiment.

The demonstration should succeed to some extent in every case. However, the most dramatic results will occur when the concentration is good—that is, when close attention is paid to the designated movements and sensations and the mood and the sensing do not wander. In other words, the quality of the awareness will determine the extent of the changes in self-perception, bodily organization and functioning.

Now take hold of your elbows with your hands, the upper arms vertical, and move your arms from left to right. Take the elbows toward the floor. Throughout the exercise, you will pay attention only to the designated movements and sensations on the *left* side of your body. Notice that the left side and the right side are executing virtually identical movements, but you will focus on the *left* side only unless told to do otherwise.

Pay attention now to the movement in your left shoulder joint. Go left to right, focusing on the movement in the left shoulder joint. Notice that there is also movement in the left elbow joint. Closely attend to that movement while maintaining awareness of the movement in the shoulder. If your head wants to go with the movement, allow it to do so, but let your awareness be exclusively of the left side of your head and neck.

Continue to note the movements and sensations in the left shoulder joint and elbow. Be sure that the movements you perform are identical on both sides. This may become increasingly difficult as there occurs a differentiation between the functional capacities of the two sides. Nevertheless, try to keep the movement the same. Now rest, placing your arms at your sides, palms down.

Allow both hands to slide down toward your feet and then back up toward your waist, keeping the two arms extended. The movement is, of course, from your shoulder joints. Pay attention to the movement in the left shoulder and the left arm and hand. Although you do exactly the same movement on the right side, pay attention only to the movement on the left.

Now stop and compare for a moment how you sense your left hand as compared to your right, your left shoulder as compared to your right, the length of the two arms.

Bend your legs so that your feet are standing on the floor, and let the legs sink first to the left and then to the right. As you do that, focus your awareness on your *left* leg. Notice that when you go left you go onto the outside of your left foot. When you come right, first the sole of the left foot contacts the floor, and as your legs continue moving to the right the inside of your left foot touches the floor. Continue the movement back and forth, noting how you move from the outside, past the sole, to the inside of your left foot.

Sense also your left knee as it describes an arc through space. Sense the movement in the left hip, and note any tendency to move farther to the left than to the right. If your movement has become more extensive to the left, equalize it so that awareness truly remains the only variable.

Try observing simultaneously the sensations experienced by the left foot, the knee and the hip. Try sensing the entire left leg as you move side to side. Is there any difference between the movements to the left and the movements to the right that now cannot be easily adjusted and equalized? Now stop.

Extend your legs and rest, observing how the legs lie. Note the contact each makes with the floor. Note the feelings of length in the two legs, and the clarity with which you perceive them.

Now let both of your feet move to the outside and bring them back to their starting point. Pay attention only to the left foot. Note that this movement is a rotation from the hip joints. Deliberately initiate the movement from the hips, rather than thinking about moving the feet. Focus your awareness on your *left* hip joint.

Notice how the *entire* left leg and foot feel. Is the movement more comfortable on one side than on the other? Is there any discomfort on one side that the other side does not experience? Again pause and rest, focusing very largely on the left side, though briefly noting ways in which it may differ from the right side.

Notice in what direction your eyes now are looking. Does your head lie on its back so that you face directly upward, or does it incline somewhat to one side?

Now bend your legs once again so that they stand on the soles of your feet. Extend your arms above you towards the ceiling and clasp your hands. Take your arms over to the left, allowing the left wrist to bend as you do so but keeping the rest of the arm extended. Then go over to the right, keeping the arm extended but bending the right wrist. However, maintain your attention on your *left* arm and the movement in the *left* wrist as you do that. Pay attention only to the left arm, and to the left side of your head and your neck if they join in the movement. And be sure that the movement is equally extensive on both sides and otherwise the same to the extent that is possible.

Now stop, and allow your palms to rest on your chest. Then bring the arms and elbows down toward your sides, and raise them back to shoulder height. Continue doing that, observing the movement in the left shoulder and arm.

Make circles with the elbows, sensing what you do on the left side. Circle clockwise and counterclockwise. Now stop, leaving your hands on your chest and your upper arms at shoulder height. Then just lift the upper arms up and down in a flapping movement, paying attention to the movement and the sensations on the left side. Now stop and rest with your hands down at your sides, palms down. Note how the left side is lying and compare that with the right side.

Rap with the backs of your knees on the floor, and focus on the bending of the left knee and its contact with the floor. Stop that and raise your hands towards the ceiling, arms extended, but wrists limp and hands and fingers dangling. And rap with the backs of the shoulders on the floor, noting the sensations in the left shoulder and the left shoulder's contact with the floor. Stop and put your arms down at your sides.

Breathe in and out and focus your attention on the breathing in your left nostril. As you focus on your left nostril, you should be able to feel the chest expanding on the left side as the lung on the left side inflates. Also sense what happens on your left side with the exhalation. Inhale and exhale, focusing on the passage of air on the left side and on any other movements on your left side involved in the breathing.

Is there movement in your left shoulder when you inhale and exhale? How much of your back on the left side is involved? As you exhale and inhale slowly, look up with your eyes when you inhale and look down with your eyes as you exhale, leaving the eyes closed and paying attention only to the movements and sensations in your left eye.

Now rap lightly with both hands on the floor. Pay attention to the feelings in the left hand. But as you do that, notice whether you hear equally the sounds made by the two hands. Or do you hear more of the sound of one hand rapping? And what happens if you deliberately decide to hear better on the left side? Now stop the rapping and slowly open your right eye and look at the ceiling. Observe what you see and also observe how much light there seems to be in the room. Then close the eye.

Slowly open the left eye. Look at the ceiling. Note how clearly you are able to see it and how much light there appears to be in the room. Closing the left eye, open the right eye again. Then close the right one and look with the left once more. Do it several times. Is there any difference in the clarity of vision and in the amount of light perceived by the two eyes? Compare your observations now with the comparison you made at the beginning.

Put your extended arms alongside your body and make your two hands into fists. Roll them outward and away from you, then bring them back toward your legs, focusing on the movement in the left hand and arm. And do the same thing with your legs. Rotate the feet to the outside and bring them back, focusing on your left side. Now make both movements simultaneously, rotating the hip joints and the shoulder joints to do it, focusing on rotations in the left hip joint and the left shoulder joint. Then stop.

Finally, bend your legs so that your feet are standing on the floor. Take the legs left and right several times, paying attention to the movement in your left foot, leg and hip joint. Is there any difference in how you move to the left and to the right?

Let your legs down. Raise your arms toward the ceiling again and clasp your hands. Let the arms go left, with your left wrist bending, and then right with your right wrist bending, paying attention to the movement in the left shoulder and the left wrist and the sensations in the left arm. Note if the movement feels the same on the left and the right sides.

Now lie quietly with your arms at your sides. Compare the contact with the floor on the two sides, the clarity of the body image on the left side and the right side, the left side of your face and the right side, your left shoulder and your right, your left hand and arm and your right, the left side of your chest and the right, and how you breathe now. Compare the left side of the pelvis and the right, the left and right legs and the feet. Then slowly roll to one side and stand up.

Sense what it feels like. Compare the contact of your feet with the floor. Notice where you want to place your weight. Do the two sides of your body feel equally alive? Walk around and compare the contact of the feet, the movement in the two shoulders. Stand still and try turning to the left and turning to the right. Note if the turning is different in one direction, more extensive, and if it feels better. Raise your left arm overhead and then your right arm. Which arm feels lighter and moves more freely?

Walk again and compare the movements in the knees and the hip joints, and observe whether the condition of one side of your body has unmistakably altered as compared to the other. If the body image is more clear on the left side, then the awareness has altered your self-perception. If your body feels longer, lighter, better on the left side, then the organization has been altered, and with that, the functioning.

As an individual learns to concentrate better, these effects increase markedly. Awareness itself is a healing force as well as a force that brings about other improvements. But it must be a positive awareness if the effects are to be positive.

In exactly the same way, a negative awareness of the self, the body, or parts of the body can impair self-perception, interfere with proper organization, cause functioning to deteriorate, and produce illness and even death. It is important to grasp the many implications of what you have just experienced.

Try to develop your understanding further, and find productive ways to apply such a fundamental and profound fact of your existence.

BODY IMAGE
AND MOVEMENT

First, lie on your back and do a body scan. As always, you look for the parts of the body that are clearest in your awareness and then those that are least clear and consider the clarity of the entire surface and the joints of your skeleton. Be aware of your two sides comparatively and notice whether you are breathing symmetrically.

Now pay particular attention to your head, neck, shoulders and upper back. People typically accumulate more tension in the upper back and neck than in other parts. Try to sense whether that is true of you.

Just let your hands roam over your face for a little while, exploring the different parts of it in such a way that your hand movements are directed *up*.

Note whether you find just a little in front of your ears and towards the top of your ears a kind of indentation in your head. Put the palms of your hands there and make rotating movements back so that you feel that it has the effect of lifting your face. Just keep the palms of the hands on those hollows and rotate the hands back. Feel that this movement lifts the face.

Now stop and put your small fingers or your middle fingers, either one, in the corners of your mouth and just gently pull out and widen the mouth a little. Pull to the left and to the right with the respective hands and feel the lips stretch and come back when you stop pulling and release. Then, instead of pulling out, use your fingers just to pull your lips *up* at the corners, towards the eyes. Just lift your lips and let them come back down.

Next, take hold of the tops of your ears and pull them up however far they easily go. Then place your hands on the top of your head and just massage it or rub it gently so that the direction of the movement is up and you feel your forehead moving up a little.

Put your arms down at your sides and sense your face, and note whether it is any more clearly in your body image, and if so, whether it is your *whole face and head* that are more clear.

Now, roll your head left to right as far as it will go. Observe whether your tongue goes with your head so that it goes from one cheek to the other, or whether it does something else. Do you sense that your eyes are immobile or that they seem to move? Now when you get to the end of any particular head movement, look a little further with your eyes in that direction. That will release the neck so that you can turn the head a little more. And if your tongue is not over on that side also, bring the tongue over and push with the tongue in the cheek as you look further with your eyes.

Then stop. Look above you and try to fix your glance on some point on the ceiling. Then, keeping your glance fixed on that point so that your eyes do not move, turn your head left to right. Sense how your head and neck movement is affected when you keep your eyes fixed at some one point above you, straight overhead.

And then let your eyes go with the movement, not looking at anything. Then stop and rest.

Now let your chin come down towards your chest, not lifting your head off the floor. Notice whether your chin makes contact with your chest. If the chin will not make contact with the chest, then open your mouth so that you can make the contact. If you have to open your mouth to do it, then notice how far you have to open it. Keep bringing the chin towards the chest and taking it away.

As you do that, be aware of the arching of the neck and try to sense clearly what is happening in the spine. Try to be aware of the space under the back of your neck, how it increases and whether you have some sense of the size of that space and the shape of it. Notice whether you breathe freely. Then stop and rest.

Now put your legs fairly close together, extended, and circle (if you can) on your tailbone, rotating your pelvis and circling without bending your legs.

Try it with your legs very slightly bent, circling on your coccyx, going in one direction for a while and then in the other direction. Then, instead of thinking of yourself as circling on the coccyx, think of yourself as circling with the pubic region. You continue to circle with the pelvis, but just think of it in that other way. Notice whether that makes any difference.

And also continue to circle with the pelvis, but think of making circles with your navel. Observe whether that affects the way the circle is made, or anything about the movement. Note whether you also can make circles with the upper part of your back at the same time that you are making circles with the pelvis. And whether you can circle with your head at the same time so that you are making three distinctly different sets of circles, circling now with the coccyx, with the back, and with the back of your head, on the floor. And note whether it is any different if you think of the circling with the pubic area and the chest and the nose. You are just thinking of the top side of your body moving instead of the back side of it while you make essentially the same kind of circles.

Now stop and rest. Let your legs be extended. Then, using your heels, rock your body up and down so that your neck moves and you can feel that when you pull, your chin comes down, and when you push, it goes away. Just allow the head to move as a consequence of being at the other end of your spine while you push and pull at the ankles. And observe how close to your chest your chin *does* come, how far back your head goes, and how much your neck arches.

Now stop and, either with your legs extended or very slightly bent, begin to circle slowly with your pelvis, having the sense that you are going around a clock and that you are going from twelve to one and two and three and four, and so on, and that you are going all the way back to twelve, but going very, very slowly, making the movement just as clear in your awareness as you can make it. If you go slowly enough with your pelvis, then you may be able to find that you can now very slowly circle with your head in the opposite direction. Do it slowly and with strong concentration. It may help to think of two clocks, being aware of the numbers, with the pelvis going clockwise and the head, counterclockwise. Go slowly. When you can do this, you will eliminate blockages in your motor cortex and there will be a "spillover" to adjacent brain areas with benefit to thinking and feeling functions.

Continue to concentrate and go very, very slowly. Try it both with your legs bent a little and with your legs extended, and note which way is easier. Be sure that you breathe freely.

Now, without thinking about what you do, circle with your head and your pelvis. Just circle, and notice what you do. Focus on circling with your pelvis, but also circle with your head. And then reverse the direction of the pelvic circling and note whether the head changes, and does so whether you want it to or not.

Stop moving and try to visualize and kinesthetically image, or image in whatever way you can, your head and your pelvis circling in opposite directions. Note whether it is possible for you to get a kinesthetic or visual image (or both) of your head and pelvis circling in opposite directions.

Then come up to a sitting position, always remembering not to get up first with your head to avoid introducing strain into neck and back muscles.

Now, put the soles of your feet together in front of you, and place your hands on the floor and circle with your pelvis again as if around a clock dial. You can think of making circles with your coccyx or with your whole pelvis. Get a clear sense of it being a *horizontal* circle on the floor.

And then circle with your head vertically so that you are making circles with your nose. See if it is not easier to do two different things with the head and pelvis now. Circle horizontally with the pelvis and vertically with the head. Be aware of whether you are going clockwise with the head or counterclockwise, or whether in one direction with the head and the other with the pelvis.

While you continue to make horizontal circles with the pelvis and vertical circles with the head, let them both go clockwise so that each one would go from twelve to one and two, and so on. Try to let both movements go in a counterclockwise direction from twelve to eleven and ten and nine, and so on, keeping the sense of one being vertical and the other horizontal.

Then note whether you can do a second different thing with the pelvis and the head, that while the pelvis circles horizontally and the head vertically, that one can move clockwise and the other counterclockwise. Notice whether it is easier or more difficult than on the floor. Go slowly. Circle, maintaining the sense of the horizontal and the vertical and taking one in a clockwise direction and the other counterclockwise, very slowly. If you can succeed with this movement, you will not only eliminate blockages but also activate higher centers in the brain because it is so far removed from what the body normally does and has done in the course of evolution. It calls forth mechanisms that are present as latencies but are not yet accessible.

Stop and rest. Remain sitting and let your hands rest wherever it feels comfortable.

Now put the feet out in front of you again and rock the body back and forth from the pelvis, the soles of the feet together and the hands behind you. Do not put pressure on the palms of your hands or you will introduce tension into the arms and neck and shoulders. The hands are there to provide balance and facilitate movement. Push the abdomen out when you go forward and suck it in when you go back. That increases the extent and ease of the movement.

Then make a few more circles very quickly. Go as quickly as you can without any feeling of compulsiveness or strain. Do a number in one direction, and then go in the other.

Then sink onto your back and make some very quick circles with your head, again without strain or compulsion, whatever are the quickest, easiest, lightest, most extensive circles you can make, changing direction more frequently than you would with the slow circles.

Then stop and take the chin towards the chest and away, and continue doing it, not picking the head up; if you have to, open the mouth to let the chin touch, and observe how much you need to do it. And if the chin now touches more easily or touches when it did not touch before, compare the movement in the neck and in the cervical spine to what you remember. In any case, compare those movements and see if now the spine is bending more in the neck.

And then just stop and rest.

Now take the head side to side again, observing how it goes, and then as you go to the left, slide the left shoulder, arm and hand down alongside your body so that the shoulder gets out of the way of the head and it can turn more. Do the same thing on the right side. Observe to what extent this allows the head to move more.

Then, continue to do the same thing, except put the palms of your hands on your chest. And see now whether the whole spine and the upper back moves much more and if the head can move more freely just by virtue of the fact that you put your hands on your chest instead of leaving them on the floor at your side. Notice how much more movement there is in the neck. Try to feel the movement the entire length of the spine. You should feel it at least down to your waist.

Then let the hands rest on the chest and just take the head side to side lightly and quickly and easily, and see how far it will go. Then stop and rest.

Now put your right hand on your forehead and use the hand to turn the head from side to side as far as it will go. Be sure that you are not turning your head in the usual way but that you are using the arm to do it, as if somebody else were turning your head. Compare that with the feeling when you are just turning your head side to side in the usual way, and see how the neck is organized. Now just turn your head from side to side and let your hand just ride along as a passenger, and compare the sensations in the neck to when you use the hand to turn it side to side.

After you have sensed clearly what it feels like to turn the head, then use the hand to turn it, and again, compare the difference. And try doing it with your left hand and see if the left hand turns it the same way that the right hand does, and if not, whether you can explain this in terms of differences in mobility of the two shoulders, or whatever other explanation you might be able to find. But note whether the left hand turns the head in the same way that the right one does and if the neck's experience is the same when the different hands are used. Let the left one just ride along the forehead and turn the head side to side. And when the sensations are clear, then turn the head with the hand again and compare it.

Now try to keep a clear awareness in memory of how the left hand turns the head, and then do it with the right one, and once again note whether there is any difference when you turn the head with the right hand and when you turn the head with the left hand, and if so, try to explain it to yourself. It will probably be in the shoulders, but there are other things that it might be. Then just stop and rest.

The rest period is always a good opportunity (whether you are asked to do it or not) to return to the body scanning position and observe the body image, particularly the part that you have been working on, noticing how it exists in your awareness and comparing that with how it existed before.

Note also your awareness of your head and compare the awareness of the neck and head with the awareness of the body below the hips, and note whether the body seems equally substantial, whether it seems bigger or smaller, denser or more refined, in some parts of the image of the body than in other parts. It is possible to bring parts of the body into such clear awareness that the rest of it will almost vanish by comparison or to create in one part of the body such a feeling of subtlety and refinement that the rest of it seems extremely coarse and dense and lumpish by comparison. The ideal is that the whole body should feel that degree of refinement and clarity, that none of it should feel coarse and lumpy or vague.

Now take the head side to side, and as you do that oppose the eye movements to the head movements, breathing freely and observing whether that affects the movement of the head. Notice where the tongue goes. Does it follow the eyes, does it follow the head when you are doing this, or does it stay neutral?

Then let the eyes go with the head. Observe that sensation and then verbalize what you are doing, as if you are instructing the head and eyes: "Head and eyes right" and then, "Head and eyes left" so that the verbalization accompanies the movement. And observe, of course, the effect of the verbal instructions or commands, suggestions, or whatever you want to call them, on the movement.

Then observe whether the head will move in response to those instructions so that it requires very little voluntary effort to turn it, either that it turns completely in response to the suggestions, or that you need to make only a minimal effort to turn it as long as the suggestions "Head and eyes right" and "Head and eyes left" are given. How much voluntary effort is required as compared to what you normally need to make? And also notice whether the movement gets smoother.

Then come up to a sitting position and try it, instructing the head and eyes to go right and then instructing them to go left, observing whether it is easier in a sitting position or a lying one. Does the head move involuntarily, or, if not, how much effort is required?

Then stop and try instructing the head to go down and then up: "Head down," "Head up." And observe whether it will move according to those instructions, or to what extent the movement has to be voluntary. Some of you will get a purely involuntary movement, some will get one that is partly involuntary and partly voluntary, for some it may be the same as it would normally be without the words. And in any case, notice whether that movement is smoother when accompanied by the verbal instructions. Note whether the chin comes down against the chest and how far back it goes, and be sure not to arch the neck excessively.

And do a few movements without verbal commands, opposing the eye movements to the head movements, breathing freely.
And then when the head comes down, let the eyelids come down
and close, and when the head goes back let the eyes roll back as far
into the head as they will easily go so that, if possible, they just float
up so that there is nothing but the whites of the eyes, but without
any sense of strain. The eyes rolling up in your head as you go up,
the lids closing as you come down.

And then just forget about the eyes. Let them do whatever they
will do, and do quick, light, easy movements up and down with the
head. Do not throw it back too much, but see if the head will just
loosely fall against your chest and if you can release the neck so that
it falls right over on your chest.

Now stop and make a few quick circles with the head, going
one way a few times and then the other way. And then sink back
down onto your right side with your legs bent a little, and as you did
before, make three distinct rotations, the pelvis rotating, the shoulders rotating and the head rotating, but now on your side. See how
fast and light and easy you can let it go. Do you remember how you
did that movement before? It is a very pleasurable movement. And
see how fast and light and easy you can let it go. One circle with the
pelvis and one with the upper body and one with the head. Note
whether you can make it in a forward direction and also if you can
make it in a backward direction. Be sure that you are really circling,
that you feel that the hip is circling, that the shoulder is circling, that
the head is circling. Bend the legs however much makes it easiest
and raise your arm however much it is easiest. Try letting the left
hand rest on the floor so that you have a clear sense of circling with
the left shoulder. Then let the back join in and the head. Circles, circling with the hip and circling with the shoulder and circling with
the head.

Then roll over on your other side and rest. Whenever you feel
like it, circle on that side with the three different segments. Notice
whether you spontaneously start to circle forward with the pelvis or
back, what you do with the shoulder and how the head goes, and
sometimes reverse it, making it just as pleasurable a movement as
you can. The whole spine should be undulating.

Then just lie on your back. Make a few circles with the pelvis,
going one way and then the other. Do some number of movements

in one direction, and then reverse it and do a number of movements in the other direction. Then do it with the pelvis and the head, also the upper back if you can.

Then just make some with the head. And stop and rest.

And continue to rest, but with your arms out at shoulder height, noticing whether you rest with your palms down or up or perhaps the hands on the side, which side it is—just what you spontaneously do—the only requirement being that they are really at shoulder height.

Maintaining the arms at shoulder height, slide the back of the head along the floor so that you bring the right ear toward the right shoulder or arm, and see if you can make contact with it or where you go. Do it several times and observe whether you can bring the ear to the shoulder. Then do it to the left and see whether you can make contact with the arm or the shoulder or not. Then leave it in the middle, having made those observations, and extend the right arm above your head against the ear. Then slide the head and the arm together to shoulder height and see if you can keep the head and the arm together. Then take it back a number of times, keeping the ear and the arm together if you can do it without strain.

Then leave the head where it is and take the arm out to shoulder height. Now take the ear over towards the arm and see if you can touch it. Do that several times. Observe whether now the ear, if it did not before, either makes contact with the shoulder or comes a good bit closer. And then leave the head in the middle and the arms at shoulder height and put the left arm up alongside the left ear, and slide them down together to shoulder height, keeping the ear with the arm if you can, breathing freely. Then leave the arm at shoulder height and take the head back into the middle and then slide it along the floor, and see if you can bring the left ear to the left shoulder.

Then take the head back and forth, bringing the ears close to the shoulder on each side, sliding the head along in the same way, sliding it from left to right with the ear touching or approaching the shoulder on each side. And if you can make easy contact with the shoulder, just sort of toss the head back and forth between the two shoulders, sliding it along the floor, but not violently, just gracefully tossing it back and forth and experiencing the movement in the neck. Do not raise the head off the floor, just let it slide back and forth from one shoulder to the other, or however close it comes.

And then rest with your arms down at your sides.

Now take the head side to side, leading the movement with your chin. And as you change the part of the body that is leading the movement, observe how the movement changes. Just turn the head side to side, thinking of leading the movement with your chin. Do it smoothly and with the greatest amount of consciousness you are able to bring to bear on it.

Then think about leading the movement with your mouth or your lips. Then continue doing it, but think of leading the movement with your nose. Then think of leading the movement with your eyes, doing it all just as consciously as possible and noting how the change in the organization that is effected by focusing on these different parts affects the movement in the head and neck.

Then think of leading the movement about at the level of your eyebrows. The eyebrows lead the movement. Turn side to side with the forehead leading the movement, a little below the hairline or where the hairline would normally be if you had one. Then still higher up on your head until you are leading the movement with the top of your head, or as close to the top where you still get a feeling of leading. Turn with the focus up at the top of the head while verbalizing "Head right" and "Head left."

Now stop for a moment. Just hold the top of your head with your hands and massage it lightly, as if you were able to reach through and touch your skull and massage the brain. And breathe up into the same space, and let the eyes float up there. And put the hands down and just continue to breathe up and through out the top of your head. Have a sense of the image doing that, and whether the head seems to elongate and what the experience of it is as you breathe into it and focus awareness up there.

Then one final time, just take the chin down towards the chest and away, and feel how much the neck arches. Take the head side to side, noticing how it moves and comparing it with how it moved at the beginning. And lie with your head in your hands a minute, the top of the head sensing up there, sensing your mouth, your lips, your eyes, the whole face and the top of the head, and the whole head and neck if you are able to, or as much of it as you can bring into the image. And then slowly roll to one side and get up and walk around and note what your experience is—the feelings of length and the weight of the body, whether it feels light, where you look, whether your visual field has expanded since the beginning—with a tendency to hold the head erect, looking out in front of you, not down at the floor. See if the head and neck feel very light and if the body below it feels light. In some cases it may even feel like the body just dangles from the head, like a kite tail, but just observe whatever your experience may be.

BODY MEDITATION

Be seated on the floor in some yoga-type position, perhaps with legs crossed and your legs resting on your feet. The ancient Egyptians sat similarly, including the famous "lotus position" of yoga. It should be a position you can stay with for a while.

Close your eyes and think about the image of a sitting yogi, or Egyptian priest or priestess, sleeping or in trance. Identify yourself with that image as best you can. Without any further suggestions about it, your consciousness will continue to alter to some degree as you immerse yourself in this exercise.

As you identify with the sleeping or in-trance magician-priest or -priestess, imagine around yourself a pyramid. Just a small pyramid, enclosing you. Take note of the shape of your body, and notice that it also now seems in the form of a pyramid. You are *meditating* and you are *inside* a small, dark pyramid. Visualize in detail and strength the image of the seated, in-trance figure, and identify yourself more and more with that image.

As you continue, consider a line running from your skull down to the base of your spine. Endeavor to visualize your spine. Try going from the skull down to the pelvis, and then from the tailbone on up to the top of the spine and skull. If it is easy to remain seated, stay in that position. If it is too difficult, then you may lie on your back as you continue.

This is a variation of an ancient exercise used in Esoteric Schools for developing internal awareness and for directing healing energies and blood flow to the parts being worked on. Visualize upward along the spine. Image the vertebrae, or imagine them, and come up to the skull.

Visualize the skull without flesh—nothing but the bones themselves. Then add to your visualization the skeleton—that part of it around the shoulders and the neck, the clavicles, the bones extending out to the side, the shoulder blades, the scapula, the back, the joints, the upper arms, the lower arms, the fingers. Add to that the visualization of the rib cage and the sternum. Continue to visualize on down to the pelvis. Then add on the hip joints and the bones of the leg and finally the feet.

Try to hold in your mind the image of the entire skeleton sitting there. Think of yourself just as that skeleton.

Then begin to flesh out the skeleton. Add muscles and ligaments as best you can. See the body without its outer covering of skin. Sense yourself to be that.

Then particularly focus awareness on the brain. Visualize the brain, the brain's hemispheres, the gray matter of the brain.

From there, in particular, try to visualize the nervous system as it extends from that brain on through the body. See, in whatever way you choose to do it, the messages flowing from the brain through the nervous system and from the body back up through the nervous system to the brain. You may see streams of continuous flowing energy or a discontinuous firing of particles of energy. Visualize this in different colors, whatever comes to you, as you sit there focusing on your brain and nervous system. Notice whether it is possible for you to feel yourself to be actually aware of the messages traveling from the brain to various parts of your body and from various parts of the body back to your brain. Sense something coming and going, back and forth, between the brain and those parts.

Then add to your imaging, or imagining, the circulation of blood, and veins and arteries, the heart pumping, the action of your lungs. Try to follow your blood streaming to those vessels and back up again. Experience the interior of yourself in this way.

Next try to see your skeleton and your muscular structure, the organs of your body, and your brain and your nervous system. See all those things simultaneously. Cover them over with skin—the covering of external flesh. Endeavor to be aware of yourself simultaneously in all of those systems. Remember and know that you are all of those things.

Voyage down inside of your body and explore it with a small ship or boat, or whatever vehicle you decide to take—something to symbolize the journey of your consciousness as it passes through the different parts of your body. Send it to the vessels of your eyes, around the different parts of your brain, down your throat, around your heart and the other organs. Let it voyage through the bones of your skeleton. Observe the functioning of the nerves. Take your own journey through yourself—the microcosmic consciousness journeying through the macrocosm of the body. Explore it as you would explore a continent or as you would explore the heavens.

Then return to the identification, for a moment, with the seated, deeply in-trance, sleeping figure inside the pyramid. Be aware of that body and merge with it. Then be aware of a subtler form of that body in yourself that is transparent and translucent, through which you can see the energy centers and the flowing and bursting of energies within. That translucent cover allows you to look completely inside and see the energy centers at the top of your head, between your eyes, at your throat, your solar plexus, your sex center, the center around the navel, and the energy flowing up and down your spine. Image, and identify with, that subtler body. Direct the energy flow to and from the different centers.

Know that in *experiencing* your body *in these different ways, at different levels of its organic reality,* and *in variations of its symbolic reality,* your brain and your unconscious mind are *acquiring the capacity* to affect different parts of your body. Know that you are establishing closer links with them so, if need be, the unconscious and the brain can quickly affect those parts and heal you more quickly and completely than you would probably be able to do otherwise.

Now, as you remain in this condition, and perhaps going still deeper, you will be introduced to an exercise which is to be done only in privacy. Lie on your back with your feet bare. Breathe in through your nose and feel yourself to exhale out through the soles of your feet. Direct the flow of breath down through the body and out through the bottoms of the feet, or breathe and image breathing so you feel that you do that. As you lie there breathing in that way, try to sense in yourself your own dying, your death, or any sickness that is sensed. With the inhalation, suggest to yourself... "Life Force in"...and with the exhalation suggest..."Death out." Allow these suggestions to coincide with the inhalations and the exhalations. Try to sense within yourself where you are dying or where you are sick—where the potential for your death is. Banish that from you with the exhalation. If you do it well, you may feel some form like a cold wind blowing out of the bottoms of your feet. Then you will know that you are making progress.

Now endeavor just once more to bring back into your awareness your skeleton, your muscles, your organs and the flowing of your blood, your breathing, your brain and your nervous system. Let your consciousness move up and down inside of yourself. Visualize, image, imagine—relate in any way that you like to those various parts. Then clothe that body once again with your external form, the flesh, the appearance that is familiar to you. Rest and deeply relax for a moment.

Then, at your own pace, stretch and breathe and, without doing it head first, sit up. Stretch again and be very, very wide awake, very, very wide awake. Feel relaxed and released and energized.

Remember what your experience was so that you can repeat it. With repetition, you will find that you will go deeper and deeper into an altered state that will allow you a more and more complete internal perception so that you will establish better contact with yourself.

You will forge those vital links between the unconscious, the brain and the other parts of the body that will allow you to self-regulate your functioning to a degree that would be impossible without some such alteration of the normal relationship and without some control over the ordinarily autonomic or involuntary processes.

Through the practice of exercises such as this, and other much more complex and complete ones, that connection with your own functioning will be enhanced. You will find it an extremely useful thing when you have need of it.

Now, once again stretch, and be wide, wide, wide *awake* in your own body, in your own skin. Feel rested and *charged,* and when it feels appropriate, get up and move around, self-observing all you can about your *whole* awareness of yourself.

INTERWEAVING SUBJECTIVE AND OBJECTIVE REALITIES

This exercise makes the point that the brain is often unable to distinguish between a subjective image and an objective percept, between a so-called subjective reality and a so-called objective reality. An "objective" experience typically occurs *in the presence* of a world known as being or existing outside and independent of any person's mind or body. Of course, all *personal experience* is subjective in the sense that it occurs only in consciousness.

Perhaps then, it is nothing to wonder at that the brain may not always differentiate between the so-called subjective and objective realities. And if you keep in mind that it is possible to present the brain with images that it will mistake for what we call actuality, then you can, by *"deceiving"* the brain, affect the body in very remarkable and profound ways.

Everyone knows that the brain, when so deceived, can carry out elaborate processes within a human body. One of the most commonplace instances that almost everyone has personal experience of is nocturnal orgasm during dreaming. The brain mistakes the dream for objective reality and triggers that whole very complex sequence of events that leads to a sexual climax. There are people who, if they can sufficiently and vividly image or even imagine sexual activity, can achieve the same thing in an awake state, or even more easily in a trance state or with certain drugs that facilitate images.

There are many other complex activities that can also be engendered by images. There is a book by the late Russian neuro-physiologist Luria called *The Mind of the Mnemonist*. It is about a patient he had who was able to image very, very vividly. If this man imaged a candle and held his hand next to it, his hand would burn. If he imaged icy water and put his hand into it, the hand became completely anesthetized. Many people in trance can demonstrate such phenomena.

The response of the body to images is undoubtedly a major factor in both illness and health, in determining when we die, how we age and so on. It is one of the reasons why there is such a great effort to change the notions about aging, including physical images, because they work as self-fulfilling prophesies. The body ages in large part according to the expectations and the images of age that people hold. If that can be reversed, then the aging process will undoubtedly move much more slowly and be much less crippling.

This exercise will be done seated and barefoot. Its purpose is to demonstrate the similar responses that the body makes to what we call actual movement and to what we call imaged movement. You should sit forward. Sit far enough forward in your chair so that your leg has freedom. If you sit too far back, you will not be able to find any of the positions where the foot moves best.

Close your eyes. Place your feet side by side, about six inches apart, so that the toes and the heels of the two feet would be on the same line if there were lines on the floor. Do it by sensing, not by looking. After you have felt the position of your feet, then look and see if the feet are in fact as you sensed them.

Again with your eyes closed, consider that you are going to rap with the balls of your feet on the floor. Place your feet where you think the rapping with the feet would be optimal, but do not rap. Just put the feet where you think you could rap best. Then, leaving your heels on the floor, actually rap with the balls of your feet. It makes a considerable difference how far your feet are placed from your upper body in determining how well you can rap with the ball of your foot. Take your feet farther away and bring them closer, and so on. Find out in what position the rapping is best done. Now keep your feet in that position where you can best rap with the balls of your feet.

In that same position, try rapping with your heels. You will find that if you really have your feet in the position where you can best rap with the balls of the feet, then you can rap only poorly with your heels. Put your feet where you can do the best rapping with your heels. Your heels should come up fairly high when you do so that the ankles flex and extend, but it is not the position where the heels can come up the very highest. Find where you can put your foot so that your heel can come up highest. You have to bring it in close to you. In this position, you will discover that you cannot lower your heel to the floor again once it has been raised. Place your feet in that relation to your body which will enable you to bring the heel up very high but will not allow you to lower it to the floor. Make a little effort, but not enough to hurt yourself, to force the foot down. Try to make your heel touch the floor.

You are going to work only with your left foot for a while. Place your left foot where you can best rap with the ball of your foot. Rap, and give your attention wholly to the movement. Then stop.

Try rapping just with your toes. You should find that the relation of the foot to the upper body is not at all so important as it is when rapping with your heels or when rapping with the balls of the feet. Still, the position where you can rap best with the ball of your foot is not the same as where you can rap best with your toes. Try to find where you can rap best with the toes.

Then bring your left foot back and rap with your heel again. The optimal position is when the ankle flexes the most and the heel comes highest into the air but yet it is still easy to lower it to the floor. Then stop and let the foot rest. Place both feet flat on the floor.

Slide the left foot forward and back, making the most extensive movement possible. Then stop when the left foot is alongside the right one. Take the ball of your left foot from side to side along the floor. Let your heel act like a hinge, and swivel your foot from the heel. Try to move the *surface* of your foot along the floor, keeping as much of the bottom of your foot on the floor as possible. Then stop.

Now, slide your left heel from side to side. Try not to pick the heel up. Then just rap lightly with your whole left foot on the floor. Pick it up and let it down lightly. Your lower leg should be at about a right angle to your upper leg. Now stop.

Close your eyes and sense your left foot. Compare it with the right foot. Note if it is clearer in your consciousness, your awareness. Notice if this is also true of your left knee, shoulder, eye, side of your mouth and face. Is the body image more clear on one side than on the other?

Extend your left leg. Leave the heel on the floor and raise the front part of the foot. Make some circles with the front part, rotating from the ankle. Make some in one direction and some in the other direction. Then stop and place the foot where you think you can most easily turn it onto its outside and onto its inside. See if you can find that place. The movement should be in the ankle. Do not take the whole leg from side to side; then the movement is in the hip joint and not in the ankle. Let your hand rest on your knee so that you can sense whether the upper leg moves or not. Do not allow the movement to be in the hip joint. Make it be in the ankle only.

Again, it will make a difference where you put your foot. Eliminate the movement from the hip joint. There will be a very slight movement in your knee, but there should not be any movement in the hip. Now stop.

Again, slide your foot back and forth along the floor. Use the foot to sense the floor. Orient yourself towards the world outside of yourself so that your intention is to sense the floor and learn everything you can about the floor. Then alter that orientation so that your interest is in your foot. Learn about *what* the foot is feeling and *how* the foot feels, *your foot's own sensations*. Then discover if you can shift smoothly back and forth between an orientation to the outer world and the inner world, self and not-self. Most people are shifting that orientation all the time, for the most part unconsciously. You also find some who are almost continuously oriented towards their own sensations and feelings. This one-sided focusing naturally makes a great difference in their thinking and behavior and what their personality is like. Sometime you might try to introspect and examine the way that you function in everyday life. Try to observe when you are oriented towards the outside and when you are oriented towards your own feelings and sensations.

Continuing to shift awareness, make circles with your foot now. Make some clockwise and some counterclockwise. When circling clockwise, try to learn about the floor. Circling counterclockwise, pay attention to yourself. Then do the opposite: continue going counterclockwise but shift your focus of attention, orienting yourself to the external world. Go clockwise and orient yourself to your own world of feelings. Then stop.

Once again, sense your two feet and the two sides of your body. Do you understand what neural re-education means? It means to alter your body image, to re-educate your sensory mechanisms. By doing these things, you alter your self-awareness in a drastic way. The body that you sense, the body of your experience, changes dramatically. Anyone with experience of Psychophysical Work will be aware of the fact that when the body image is sharpest, then the functioning is also best. However, the body image must be in coincidence with the physical body or else the action taken is not the action that one thinks one is taking. Clarity of body image alone is not enough. It has to be a correct body image, coinciding with the actual physical body. All this is absolutely *basic* to *psychospiritual* as well as psychophysical development.

Now rap a few more times with your left heel. Place it where the movement is optimal. Then place your foot where you can best rap with the ball of the foot. Next place it where you can best rap with the toes. Flex and extend the toes. Place the foot where it is quick and light and easy to do.

Slide your foot back and forth a few times. Stop when your feet are symmetrical in their positioning.

Get up and walk around for a while. Compare the contact the left foot makes with the floor with the contact the right foot makes. Which foot is more flexible? Ascertain if your left knee moves differently than your right one. Also discern if there is any difference between the two shoulders. Then come back and sit down.

The differences in sensing and functioning have been achieved by means of movements accompanied by awareness of the movements, by focusing on the sensing. To the extent that movements have been done with awareness and focused sensing, your left foot should be well differentiated from your right foot, and your body image should be clearer on the left side. Your entire left side, not just your foot, should function better comparatively.

Now the question arises whether the brain will alter the body to the same extent if you only imagine or image the movements. If the body is altered to the same or a greater extent by means of images alone, then presumably that means that the brain either cannot differentiate between the imaged movement and the actual movement, or it does not care one way or another. The fact probably is that it is not able to differentiate.

Close your eyes and try to get a clear image of your right foot. You will probably find it difficult because the left foot is now much clearer than the right one. In some cases, the right foot will hardly seem to be there at all. In fact, if you differentiate enough, the sensing of one side of the body will disappear completely, or almost so.

Now, with each of the following instructions, perform a couple of movements, not the many you did on the left side. This will give you an actual experience of the sensations involved in the movements. Then you will imagine or image the movement, whichever you are able to do. Three kinds of images, or imagination, will be involved here. For our purposes, the most important of these is kinesthetic images. That is the feeling of the movement itself. The second is tactile images, which means the sense of touch, the contact that the foot makes with the floor. In this case, the contact of the foot with the floor is what you will be imagining mostly. Thirdly, use visual imagination or imaging, knowing what the movement looks like. By using all three of these, you will create a much more complete reality than if you used only visual imagery or only kinesthetic imagery.

Place your right foot where you think you can do the best rapping with your heel. Rap just a couple of times. Then stop and, drawing upon the sensing that you just did, about 15 times imagine or image the rapping. Try to make the sensory powers of your imagination so strong that you can truly feel it. Now continue to imagine rapping with the heel, or to image it.

Pay close attention to what you are doing. Note if it is harder work to image the movement than it is to actually perform it. You would think that something done in the mind would be easier. However, note if you do not feel the imaging of the movement to be more difficult. Do you tend to interfere with your breathing, or to tighten your shoulders and neck muscles, or to do various other things that make the imagined movements hard work?

Now imagine some movements with the left heel rapping. Observe what you do with your body. Then stop and do a few actual movements with your left heel. Notice if, as soon as you start doing the actual movements, the tension lets go and the thing becomes comparatively very easy. The physical movement is easier than the imaginary movement so long as the imagination, the imaging faculties, have not been cultivated. When they are untrained, then the imagined movement is harder. Now stop.

Again imagine rapping with the right heel. Try not to tense your shoulders, neck and face. Do not hold your breath. Also observe, as you imagine that just as vividly as possible, whether you can feel the tendency in your right heel to rise and whether, perhaps, you actually do move it a little bit. In fact, when you imagine any movement, there are measurable micro-movements, very small movements, made by the muscles in response to the images. Observe whether you can be aware of that. Also, note if you can be aware, or if it seems to you that you are aware, that your brain is sending those signals down to your foot to raise and lower your heel. Then if you sense actual movement in the heel, try to sense the signals also coming back to the brain. Determine if you notice that when you inhale your heel tends to come up a little bit, and when you exhale it goes down. Observe if the same thing happens with your shoulders and other parts of your body, rising and falling with the exhalation and the inhalation.

Now actually put your right foot out where you think you can rap best with the ball of the foot. Do it two or three times and note carefully the sensations. Then stop and imagine it. Do the actual physical movement only two or three times so that it is not enough to substantially affect the results. It is just to give you something to work with in your imagination since you are not able yet to imagine those movements well enough otherwise. Imagine rapping. Imagine it very vividly and try not to do those things with your body that make the imagining physically difficult.

Now, observing closely, rap two or three times with your toes. Then continue imagining doing that. Next slide the entire foot from side to side, then imagine sliding it. Imagine the contact of the foot with the floor in that side-to-side sliding movement. Now actually slide the foot forward and backward a couple of times. Observe your movement and sensations, and then imagine repeating that movement 25 times. Imagine it very vividly, and again orient yourself towards learning about the surface beneath your foot for about ten movements. Then switch the orientation towards your own feelings for ten movements. Then stop and rest a minute.

If you have allowed your hands to move, place them on your thighs, palms down. You should sit far enough forward so that your body can be upright and your fingers can rest easily on your knees without your bending.

Move the ball of your right foot from side to side a couple of times, using the heel as a hinge. Stop and imagine doing it. Remember to make the imaging easy, avoiding those tensions that make it difficult. With practice it becomes easy, and the images may acquire a transformative power that exceeds that of actual movement.

Now do a couple of movements taking your right heel from side to side. Note those sensations. Then do that movement in your imagination. Remember to use the kinesthetic, the tactile and the visual sensory imaginations. Now stop and rest with your hands on the knees.

Compare your two feet for a moment. Note which is clearer in your body image, and also which knee, which hip joint, which shoulder and which side of the face has more clarity. Observe if this is a difference from before.

Remain seated about halfway forward on your chair. Now extend your right leg out to where you think you can most easily turn it onto its outside and onto its inside. Perform the actual movements several times. Then continue to do it with your imagination—kinesthetic, tactile and visual. Now stop.

Pick your right foot up and put it down lightly several times. Then continue to imagine doing that. Next make several actual circles with your feet on the floor, two clockwise and two counterclockwise. As you alternate the direction of the circles, also alternate your orientation between self and not-self. Learn about the floor, and then learn about the feelings in the foot. Such shifts in reality orientations are particularly potent in strengthening the neural circuitry.

Now, drawing on past experience and without doing any actual movements, image sliding the foot back and forth. Again, switch the orientation back and forth between the so-called objective and subjective realities. Imagine pressing hard so that you sense clearly what the floor feels like and the sensations in the bottoms of your feet are stimulated. Now stop.

Again, without actually moving, remember the sensation of rapping your heel, and in your imagination rap with your right heel on the floor. Imagine it very strongly and note any tendency of your heel to rise. You might notice a shift in the pressure of your toes on the floor.

Then put your foot where you think you can best rap with the balls of your feet. Imagine that movement. Imagine doing it very quickly with your ankle flexing a lot. Make it light but vigorous and rapid rapping.

Then imagine rapping with your toes. Bring them up as high as you can, in your imagination only. Then, just a few more times imagine sliding the foot forward and backward along the floor.

Note if you can simultaneously and *equally* sense the floor and the feelings in your foot. Notice whether it seems to you that your orientation is more towards the floor or towards the foot. Now stop.

Keep your eyes closed and observe which hand you sense more clearly as well as which foot, shoulder, elbow, knee, ankle and which side of your face.

Open your eyes and walk around. Observe whether now it is the right side that moves better, the right foot having a better contact with the floor. Is your right knee more flexible? Determine whether the change is the same from the imaginary or imaged movement, as compared to the changes resulting from actual, physical movement. Is the change greater, or is it less? Ascertain if there is some kind of qualitative difference in your experience of the body; is there a different sensuous quality from imaging than from the actual movement? It is a subtle discrimination that you should try to make, to find what the difference is between what is achieved by the imaging and what is achieved by the movement. Then sit down.

Now close your eyes and put your feet side by side. Can you sense much more clearly your right foot and the right side of your body? Now you will equalize the two sides.

First, rap with both heels on the floor. Place your heels where they rap well, and determine if one raps faster than the other. Then put your feet where the balls rap best and rap them. Then rap with your toes. Use all of your toes, if you can do it.

Then put your feet where you can rap best with your heels, and *imagine* rapping both heels at once. Imagine doing so as vividly as you can. Now place your feet wherever you can rap best with the balls of your feet, and imagine doing that. Next, using all three varieties of imaging—kinesthetic, tactile and visual—continue to image rapping. Then place your feet where you can best rap with your toes, and imagine rapping them.

Then swivel the balls of both feet simultaneously left and right five times. Swivel in the same direction, right to left. Then imagine doing it.

Now stop that and actually slide your heels left to right, sliding the feet along the floor. Let them move equally and symmetrically. Sense clearly what you are doing, where the movement is. Then imagine doing it.

Now again, physically move your feet by sliding them forward and backward along the floor. As you do that, alternate between awareness of the floor and awareness of the feelings in your feet. Do a number of movements sensing outward and a number of movements sensing inward. These are all misleading ways of speaking, but the language does not really allow for an accurate description. You may understand, but it is not adequate language because that language is so geared to a too simple differentiation between the "subjective" and the "objective" world when it comes to describing things like movement and sensing.

Now circle with your feet on the floor, some clockwise and some counterclockwise. Now with one foot sense the floor, and with the other foot pay attention to the feelings in the foot. One foot is outer-directed and one foot is inner-directed. When you change the direction of the circling, also change what the foot is doing so that if it was the left foot that was outer-directed now it is the left foot that is inner- directed, and the reverse. Do that a number of times, changing both the direction of the circling and the orientations of the respective feet. Then imagine doing it. Breathe freely and do not become tense. And now stop.

Sit with your hands resting lightly on your knees, your body erect. Close your eyes and note whether you sense equally your two feet, your two hands. Does it seem to you that your nose is in the middle of your face if it normally feels so? If you still sense one side more clearly, work both physically and in the imagination on the side where the image is faintest to make it as vivid as it is on the side where it is strongest. Do it with movements of your foot, the kinds of movements we have been doing. Choose your own movements, and choose to what extent you do these as actual physical movements and to what extent you do them as imaged movements, provided you do some of both. When you feel that the two sides of the body are equally clear, that your body image is the same on both sides so that it is a balanced body image, then get up and move around. Determine if the two sides are in fact equal. Do it well, with regard to what you sense you need. Now sit down.

You have seen *that the mind can use the brain* by means of sensory images to reorganize and change those functions of the body *of which it has some experience.* Now you can, at this point, use the mind and its images to cause the brain to reorganize the body so long as you have knowledge of the sensations that are involved. You have to consciously know what the sensations are in order to image them before you can exert any conscious control over the organism itself in the way that you were doing. There are also many processes of the body *that you are not able to sense.* To the extent that you are able to increase the range of your sensing, to sense inward and to actually acquire some sensory knowledge of internal processes, then you can bring those under conscious control as well. Otherwise, they can only be controlled through some kind of collaboration with the unconscious. To control such things as heart rate and skin temperature and blood flow and brain waves and other ordinarily involuntary processes, it is really only necessary to establish a relationship with your unconscious mind that will take advantage of the knowledge your unconscious has of how to use the brain to regulate those involuntary mechanisms and processes. It is a somewhat dangerous and haphazard process as compared to establishing conscious control. Therefore, the range of conscious experience should be made as great as possible. *The sensing and the conscious awareness should penetrate as far into the body, as deeply and as completely as possible,* so that the conscious mind can be used to bring about any of the changes that you want to bring about. Beyond that, you can only work with your unconscious and ask it to do these things for you. You can accomplish this by forming some kind of effective relationship between the unconscious and the brain.

At the beginning and throughout this exercise, the point has been to show that your brain does not in many instances discriminate between images and objective actions. When you observe the changes that occur in your body, regardless of whether you do the imaginary or the actual physical movement, you understand that your brain does *not* distinguish. *Your body will also alter profoundly—and more mysteriously—in response to symbols,* but that is another matter.

MINDFULNESS:
WALK AND STOP!

The following exercise—or some variation of it—is extremely ancient and has been taught in many esoteric Schools throughout known history. It is very useful and also easy to remember how to do. It should be done at least once a week and provides a means whereby a student can measure his/her progress in mindfulness by comparing the present experience with past ones.

In essence, awareness is increased part by part, function by function, sensation by sensation, everything being done slowly and carefully and with the emphasis always on *quality of consciousness.* And now to begin.

In this exercise, you will walk as mindfully as possible, bringing your entire body into awareness as the exercise progresses. When you hear "Stop!," no matter what position you are in, you will freeze and examine your body image in its entirety as best you are able to do it. The idea is to *freeze* the movement and to observe yourself *exactly as you are at the moment of the Stop!* and to compare your observations to what you thought you were doing at the time. Repeated Stops give you a chance to re-examine yourself and note whether you make the same observations about yourself that you had made earlier.

Begin walking, bringing your whole body into awareness as best you can. Then note the contact of your feet with the floor, what part touches the floor first, second, and third, and whether the heel comes down and you travel over the bottom of the foot, the toes then leaving the floor in the order of their length. Observe next the feeling in your ankles, and then expand your attention to include aware- ness of your lower legs. Bring your knees into your body image so that your feet, toes, ankles and knees should *all* be within your field of awareness. Stop!

Examine exactly what you are aware of, not only those parts to which your attention has been directed, but the totality of your awareness, including emotions, ideas, images, and sensations, but particularly your awareness of your body.

Resume walking, maintaining as much as possible of your awareness of your lower legs especially. Bring your upper legs into awareness, the hip joints and then your pelvis, trying to hold every- thing below your navel within your awareness very clearly. Stop!

Again, try to examine exactly what is in your consciousness.

Walk again, being aware very fully of your body at least up to your navel, and bring into that field of awareness hands and wrists, lower arms and elbows, and become aware, too, of your upper body—the front of it, the back, and the sides, without sacrificing or diluting anything that you were aware of before. Add the upper arms and shoulders. Stop!

Continue moving, continuously self-observing what is in your awareness, particularly whether with everything that you are doing with your body you sense the movement in all of your joints and on the surface of your body. Know as fully and exactly as possible what you are doing with your feet and legs and arms, pelvis and upper body, bringing in the neck, and be sure that if anything slips away, you restore it. Stop!

Observe also whether it is easier or more difficult to be aware of your body when moving or standing still and whether the thoughts and the emotions or anything else change when you are moving or motionless. Compare your observations during this Stop! to those you made the last time.

Continue to move, allowing your head and neck to come into the body image fully if they are not already there so that you sense clearly what you are doing with your mouth and eyes and breath- ing. Sense how your head is being held, and your neck, and from the bottoms of your feet to the top of your head. Observe whatever may be missing and try to bring it in. Stop!

Try to be aware of whether your sense of time is any different when you are moving or when stationary. Note if, when stopped, there is any difference in your awareness of time, space, or any parts or all of your environment. Maintain awareness of your physical sensations and also of the body of thoughts and emotions.

Begin to move again, being aware of time and space and environment, and compare your awareness in motion to your awareness during the previous Stop period. Stop!

Once again, observe: remember what was in your consciousness while moving, and be aware of what is in your consciousness now. Compare your observations.

Continue walking, and notice whether, while retaining a full awareness of yourself, you are able to observe others without sacrificing the self-awareness. How much of your consciousness can you give to the observing of other things, and what can you observe?

A high level of mindfulness is clearly in large measure useless if it prohibits being mindful of the world outside oneself. Be able to be self-aware and at the same time bring a high level of observation to what is external to you, particularly, of course, to what is relevant. Be able to focus on a few perceptions or expand the field so that you can be aware of everything that is around you without sacrificing self-awareness. Try to hold in mind what it is that you have been observing around you, how you have observed other people or objects while self-remembering. Stop!

Note what is in your consciousness now as compared to what was in your consciousness the last time you Stopped. Ascertain whether you have added more to the consciousness. If so, was it without sacrificing what was there before, or did you allow something to slip away in order to add something else?

Now, continue to move, self-observing, self-remembering all sensations, all movements, feelings, thoughts and images. At the same time, endeavor to look at whatever is around you in the manner of a highly skilled or highly trained observer. Try to see everything about the people you observe, without sacrificing awareness of yourself.

Look at them as if to observe as many of their movements as possible, *discerning from the movements what the sensations are*. Notice how your body is held, the expression on your face, the body language. Also discern the emotions of the person you look at, and notice to what extent you feel that you are aware of the thoughts occurring inside that person.

Note whether such observation makes a difference in what you see, and compare your observations now to the ones you make habitually. Even as you do this, continue to maintain your full mindfulness of yourself. Note whether it seems to you to be very easy to tell what is going on inside of some people, and whether others are a little more difficult. Do you detect in yourself any tendency to hide now that you know how intensely you are being observed, any tendency to put on masks or alter your way of being in order to be for others rather than for yourself? Stop!

Again walk around very carefully, observing others as well as yourself. Notice if you alter anything about yourself because you are being observed so closely. Know that it may be possible to look at you and know what your emotions, thoughts, and sensations are, what the condition of your being is as reflected and made clear by your movements, posture and body language. Ascertain if you truly can maintain all these things in your field of awareness without sacrificing your self-remembering, and having discovered that you have sacrificed some of it, get it back. Stop!

In the Stop position, bring your entire body and self just as fully into awareness as you possibly can, scanning from your feet to the top of your head, bringing in anything that needs to be brought in. Also be aware of feelings, emotions, thoughts, sensations and, if you can sense it, your quality of being, your spirit. Notice if you can get a different sense of your own level of being and self-actualization—to what extent you have approached what you might be and to what extent you are aware of the gap between what you are and what you might be. The more you self-remember and self-observe, the clearer that gulf is likely to become, making it easier eventually to close it.

Once more, walk around, sensing yourself completely and in totality, not just body. Then return to your starting place and sit down as mindfully as possible, keeping in awareness as much as you can of what you were able to achieve during this exercise.

Examining The "I"

Begin by just comfortably standing. Consider the fact that when a person refers to his or her "I"—not the "e-y-e" but the capital letter "I," the self—in different cultures the tendency is to locate it in different parts of the body.

In some cases, the person, when he/she refers to his/her "I," will seem to be speaking from the head; in other cultures, from the heart; and in yet other cultures, from the belly. This is curious because when you talk about yourself you should have a feeling of speaking about the *whole of yourself* rather than just some part of yourself.

In the case of the person who says "I am this or that" and experiences the "I" as being mainly in the head, it may seem that it is the brain that is speaking and the proximity to the brain has something to do with it. But why the perception of speaking from the heart or the belly? And yet those are very common experiences in other cultures.

In this exercise we will explore whether seeming to speak from one part or another of the body only applies in special circumstances. Begin by simply stating silently to yourself, "I am, I am," and you can use your name, "I am John Jones" or "I am Mary Smith," and "I am going to visit my friend" or "I am going to Paris tomorrow."

133

Notice if you localize your "I" in some part of your body. If you do, does it make any difference whether you say those different things? Repeat those statements for a while and notice what you observe.

Now repeat them with your eyes open and also repeat the words with your eyes closed, and note if that makes any difference.

And repeat simply, "I, I, I," understanding that you are referring to yourself. Again repeat that with your eyes open and then do it with your eyes closed, and note your experience.

If you think that you are not localizing "I" in any part of your body, observe very closely and see if in fact that "I" is as much in one part as in another. When you are saying "I," is it as much in your left hand as in your right shoulder, in your left knee as in your right foot? As much on the front and back of your body, on the sides and in the armpits as it is, say, in the head?

Now sit down and continue repeating "I, I, I." Notice whether it makes any difference whether you are standing or sitting, whether the experience of speaking of yourself is affected by the actual position of your body. Now change the reference to yourself a few times, using such words as "myself," "me," perhaps your name, and notice whether those experiences are all the same with respect to the parts of your body the words most directly relate to.

Speak your name, your first name, a few times so that it definitely refers to you. Then speak it merely as a name that is the name of many people and does not belong to anyone in particular. Note whether your sense of identity is affected by that.

Lie with your face down and repeat "I" many times.

Note whether you feel that same part of yourself when you say "I" when you are lying on your stomach as when you stand or sit. Is the experience the same or different?

When a person refers to him- or herself and experiences him- or herself as existing more in one part of the body than in other parts, that indicates a certain amount of alienation from the body, and perhaps from the self in other ways. Ideally, when you speak of yourself, you mean all of yourself. You are then as conscious of one part of yourself as you are of any other.

Observe yourself closely and do a body scan. Sense your body image and determine what parts are in your awareness clearly, what parts are less clear, and what parts are not there at all.

When you have finished body scanning, again speak the words

"I" and "I am" and "I'm going to do this" and "I've done that." Note whether you speak for more of yourself or are still as localized as at the start and in the same way.

If you observe closely, you will notice that there are two different experiences—sensing the body and defining oneself in terms of the body.

It is possible, even when one is unable to sense the body clearly, to refer to one's whole physical self with the word "I" or its variations. The way you know you are doing that is if you don't feel any sense of localization when you speak the word "I."

There are very few people who can speak of themselves without referring to any body at all, any physical body. These are usually schizophrenics who may believe that they have no physical body, who don't experience one, or if they do experience it, it is "dead." There are also some peculiar cults and spiritual practices where one deliberately detaches the "I" from the body with the aim of not being distracted by giving in to it.

Roll to one side and stand up. Continue to speak words of reference to yourself, observing with your eyes closed and with your eyes open. Try to sense what happens when you say to yourself, "My right hand. This is my right hand." Notice that in fact calling attention to your right hand makes a difference in the experience of your right hand and your self-awareness. Simultaneously think "I" and "My right hand." If you localized it before in your head, note whether now your head *and your hand* are more represented by the statement "I" than other parts of your body, and that the hand is also *sensed more clearly*. Does that right hand that is "my hand" actually seem more "my hand" than the left one does? Sense that. Do the same thing asserting, "This is my left foot. This left foot is mine. I am my left foot, along with other parts of me. I am my left foot, my left foot is mine. I am my left foot." Think at the same time "I," "I am," "My left foot is mine."

Continue to affirm and insist and declare "This is my left foot," and note that as you do so the left foot does seem to be more yours than your right foot. Become more identified with it, sense it differently, know that it is more present in your awareness when you refer to yourself than other parts of you.

Now, imagine yourself walking. Say to yourself, "I am walking. This is me walking." Notice whether you sense your body to be engaged in walking. Notice also whether it makes any difference when you repeat to yourself the "I," then the "me," and then your name.

Does it make any difference in the localization of the "I" whether you speak of yourself standing or walking? You will have to pay very close attention.

Imagine yourself swimming in comfortably cold water. Notice the water on your skin. Note where your "I" is.

If there is more than one person present, sit down and face one another. Otherwise, imagine there is more than one person present. Look at one another while repeating "I" in the same way. Note the effect of affirming the "I" in this situation. Does it remain in the same part of your body? Is it the same or stronger? Notice the sense of yourself that you now have.

Now stop looking at the other person or imagining the other's presence, and close your eyes. Continue repeating the "I," "I am," and the name referring to yourself. Then think of yourself as being completely alone. Affirm your own existence in the way that you have been doing. Pay close attention.

Now imagine that there are 20 people looking directly at you. Is your experience of your "I" affected by that? They are all watching you carefully and looking directly at you.

Imagine that there are five people doing that. You are repeating your "I" and those five people are looking directly at you. You don't know anything about what is going on in their minds. All you know is that they are looking at you and you are saying your "I."

Imagine that there are ten people ringed around you. You are standing in front of 100 people or sitting in front of 100 people. Does it make any difference to your self, your "I," to the way the "I" represents you, or the way your "I" refers to your body?

Does it make any difference if it is a larger number—500 or a thousand? Affirm your "I" and observe yourself, and then as you do the "I" repetitions, just be completely alone again.

Note whether your experience of the "I" is the same as when you began or whether it refers to more of you or less of you or has changed in any other way. Continue to use the word "I" to refer to yourself, including your body, as you open your eyes and look at the person opposite you or the person you imagine to be opposite you. Again, note whether there is a difference. What does the "I" refer to?

Be certain as you do say "I" that you look at the other person and are aware of the person opposite you. Observe whether it is any different if you close your eyes yet continue to think of yourself as looking at the other person and the other person as looking at you. Continue to affirm your "I."

Paying careful attention, once again think of yourself as being alone. Continue to affirm your "I." Does that make any difference to what you feel physically or otherwise?

Lie on your back a minute and continue affirming your "I." Compare your conscious awareness of what you experienced sitting with what you experienced lying down before. Notice whether lying down refers to more of you or less of you, or whether it is the same.

Slowly roll to one side and stand up, trying to recall how you stood when we first began. Stand the same way or as close to the way you were standing after you first thought about yourself in relation to the word "I." Speak it, "I," "I am," "me," "myself," and your name, referring to yourself.

Now repeat simply the "I," and note whether the reference is the same as it was in the beginning of the exercise. Has anything changed? If so, what is it?

Slowly walk around, affirming your "I." Pay the closest possible attention to the awareness you have of your body, using your senses. Endeavor to bring every part of your body into sensory awareness as you walk.

Notice the contact of your feet with the floor, the movements in your ankles, knees, and hips, what you do with your arms, shoulders, neck and head while you repeatedly affirm your "I."

You are doing two quite distinct activities. Sense carefully your body as you walk, and be at the same time as mindful as possible of how the "I" reference to the body is affected.

Do you sense clearly your movements? Your contact with the floor? The contact of different body parts brushing against each other? Can you still maintain your awareness of these sensations while localizing your "I," for example, in the head? If you can do that and if you normally do it, your self is alienated from your body. Consciousness must be split in order to know that one is moving and sensing certain things and yet still be thinking of oneself as being only a part or parts.

Now just stand in what you think is your normal way and close your eyes. Repeat "I" and your name, and "I" and your name, and observe if any more of your body seems to be represented when you say the word "I" than at the beginning of the exercise. Now, sit down and rest.

This particular type of self-observing and self-remembering is also a form of meditation or practice of concentration. If you continue to practice, you will gradually find that more and more of yourself will be referred to when you say the word "I" or refer to yourself in some other way. You will be identified consciously with what is closer to the totality of yourself than people usually ever are. Finally, with sufficient work, the *entirety of yourself* will be included when you say "I." With practice, you will overcome conflicts within yourself that result from alienation from your body. This can also be achieved with respect to thinking, feeling, or emotions. That is another step beyond what you are doing here now. In the ideal case, the "I" would refer to one's whole self or whole being.

It is a good thing to observe, for at least a while each day, what you are referring to when you refer to yourself. It is one means towards real self-knowledge.

ENTERING THE SILENCE

All major systems of meditation, and other ways of growth and self-actualization, recognize the very great importance of quieting the mind—of bringing an end to the customary inner noise, the babble and chatter and chaotic flow of ideas and images from the unconscious which reduces so much of waking life to a dismal parody of true awareness—of real waking states and genuine autonomy.

The necessity is clear, but the task is very, very difficult—for many, impossible. Those who have struggled to "empty the mind," to enter into and remain in a silence free of images, ideas and sensations, know just how very difficult. However, it may be that there are methods and techniques not known to, or adequately used by, most teachers. We will explore that possibility here in this lesson.

There are a pair of simple but important facts—research findings—in which this lesson is grounded. These are that the occurrence of verbal ideation requires at least minute collaboration—movement—of the apparatus of speech, while for the person to experience images, there must be at least some slight tension and movement, however miniscule, of the eyes. If the vocal apparatus and the eyes are sufficiently relaxed to inhibit their movement, then neither verbal ideation nor imagistic thinking can occur.

With these preliminaries, you now will attempt to determine to what extent you will be able to enter the silence, quiet the inner noise

and chatter, by achieving a profound relaxation—including a relaxation of parts of the body not ordinarily included in any relaxation procedures. In fact, those knowledgeable in meditative techniques now may learn something valuable about ways in which
these methods are deficient.

And now, lie on your back, with your eyes opened or closed as
you prefer, and sense your body very closely, starting with your
toes.

Beginning with your toes, scan your body for tension, releasing
the tension from any part where you find it. If you have difficulty
releasing the tension from, say, the toes, then it should be helpful to
flex the toes, make them even more tense, and then let go of that *in-
duced* tension, and of the other tension with it. Tense and let go, tense
and let go. Do the same with any other muscles where you have
trouble releasing the tension you experience. Do that until you are
just as relaxed as possible. Scan your body on up to your chest. Then
go back down to your hands and your arms and back up your arms
to your shoulders. Finally, relax the neck, face and head. As you do
this, note where you encounter the tension and where you are able
to get rid of all of it, most of it, some of it, little or none of it, so you
will remember all that later.

Observe whether you notice any tension in your buttocks. If
there is usually a little indentation of the side of the buttocks, then
you have tension there whether you know it or not. Tense the buttocks and then release them, bouncing yourself up and down. Contract and let go, contract and let go—that will bounce your body up
and down. You do it most effectively by rapidly clenching and un-
clenching the muscles of the buttocks. The buttocks alone should
bounce the body, without any help from the legs. Do it as quickly
and lightly as possible, and then stop without becoming fatigued.

As you go through the entire relaxation process—now or on
other occasions—verbalize what it is you want of your body so that
you develop a capacity to talk to your body, and your body will respond. Over a period of time it will learn to make better and better
responses. Couple the suggestion that some particular muscles are
going to release with the actual experience of releasing those muscles. For example, say, "buttocks release" at the same time you experience the release. Similarly, say to yourself, "hips release," "pelvis
release," "ankles release," "knees release," "chest release," "shoulders release," and so on. And say, "Toes and feet lengthening and

loosening," "fingers and hands lengthening and loosening." Or, "Neck free," "back lengthening and widening." Give yourself many of these verbal suggestions, and later on you will find you have reached a condition where your body will respond to those suggestions or orders. As you learn to so respond, the muscles will stop contracting and will lengthen, becoming longer as you talk to them. And the joints will release, as when you suggest to yourself, "Shoulder joints releasing," and "elbows," and "wrists," "hip joints," "knees," and "ankles releasing," and so on.

While you are working on establishing that capability of talking to your body so that it will do what you suggest it will do, you must refrain from making any movements. Once you begin to work with suggestions alone, you must not consciously move to carry out the suggestion—let your body-mind's response occur involuntarily. There may be very few limits to how far you can go in creating a capacity of your body to respond to such suggestions. We know that by such means you can gain control of blood flow, skin temperature, even heartbeat. Still more profound responses are possible, with some possibilities for self-regulation and self-healing exceeding anything presently achieved by any known methods, however sophisticated.

And now, as you lie on your back, inhale fairly deeply and then retain the air. What inflates more—your chest or your abdomen? As you hold your breath, push the air back and forth between your chest and your belly in a kind of seesaw movement. Move it back and forth as many times as you can while holding your breath without discomfort. When you need to exhale, do so with a hiss. Put your tongue between your teeth and hiss as you exhale. Do it several times—inhale, push the air back and forth between chest and belly, and then exhale with a hiss. Feel your shoulders and your back settling to the floor as you hiss. Continue repeating these movements. The hissing helps your body to relax, it lets you settle more closely to the floor.

Now continue with the relaxation process, moving on up to your shoulders, and relax them until you are ready to start working on your neck, releasing tensions from your neck. Remember, the instructions to the joints are to release, the instructions to the muscles are to lengthen. Be sure not to hold your breath as you continue to relax more and more. It is difficult to relax effectively if at the same time you hold your breath.

Now as you focus your awareness on your neck and your head, give yourself the suggestion, "neck free, neck free," "jaw releasing," "face releasing," "back lengthening and widening."

Try to notice whether the tension in the neck increases or diminishes when you inhale and when you exhale. Is it more relaxed when you inhale or when you exhale? Notice whether your impression about this remains constant over a number of sets of inhalations-exhalations. Do you become more tense in the neck as you seek an answer to that question? Distinguish between any tension resulting from trying too hard to pay attention to yourself and alterations of tension as you breathe which are due just to the breathing. Suggest to yourself, "neck free, neck free," and note if you can detect a response from your body.

Now continue and relax the rest—the face and head. Check the jaw again and observe whether there is any tension in the jaw. Thrust the lower jaw forward several times so that the lower teeth go outside the upper lip. Then open your mouth wide, and the jaw is more free. How about your tongue? How does your tongue lie? When you are sitting up, the tongue, if relaxed, will lie flat on the floor of your mouth. When you lie down, the relaxed tongue is still close to the floor of your mouth, although it may not be touching it. Stick out your tongue as far as you can, straight in front of you. Do not wiggle it, just stick it straight out and hold it there a minute. Then bring it back into your mouth and allow it to relax. Do that several times, holding it tense a minute, and then giving it time to relax inside your mouth. Also, push a few times with your tongue against the roof of your mouth, then stop pushing and allow the tongue to relax. As the tension goes out of the tongue, do you also note that some tension goes out of the throat, perhaps out of the face as well?

Try pushing your tongue against the roof of your mouth, then letting go a few more times. You can also push against the floor of the mouth with the tongue, and then let go—let the tension just go out. Now stick the tongue out stiffly before bringing it back in. Continue sticking your tongue out, taking time to allow your tongue to relax before you stick it out again. Relax as well the other muscles you may sense as involved in that activity: the neck muscles, the facial muscles, the muscles around the mouth especially. Give them all a chance to relax. There are also muscles in the back of the neck that tense up when you stick your tongue way out. Try to feel them, and let go of every bit of the tension. How does your tongue lie now? Does it feel wider now?

Let the tongue, the neck, the mouth and the face go limp and loose, and forget about them for a while. With your eyes closed, observe whether you can feel clearly the weight of your eyeballs. Now, for a little while, imagine that you are watching a ping-pong game. You are somewhere near the middle of the table and you are watching the ball being hit back and forth from one end of the table to the other. Be certain you breathe freely as you watch. Then, instead of watching ping-pong, watch a tennis game. You are looking over a much greater area as the ball travels back and forth. Be very conscious of the movement of your eyes for a while. Let them move as they wish while watching the game, but be conscious of the movement.

Stop watching the tennis game and look towards your toes. Then look up towards the top of your head. Down and up, down and up, and do it a number of times. Then stop that and, still with your eyes closed, think that you are looking at the ceiling and that you can turn your eyes around in your head and look down at the floor. Look at the ceiling, and then just look at the inside of your eyelids. Look at the ceiling, and then at the eyelids. Then turn your eyes around in your head so that you can look through the back of your head at the floor. Imagine doing that, and breathe freely all the while—all the while being very conscious of your eyes, of what your eyes are doing and how they feel as they carry out these various tasks, these various exercises.

Now, envision an automobile driving along a road. Notice whether you can see the automobile moving along the road, and note how it is moving across your field of vision—is it from left to right, from right to left, or some other way? Stop looking at that.

Now look at someone riding a horse. Imagine that or, better, image it. How is the horse moving?—in what direction?—and who is riding the horse, if anyone? Now stop and look at someone who is walking. See someone walking and observe closely, taking in as much detail as possible. Notice whether the figure is walking, and be aware also of how your eyes move. Determine if you can both watch the walking figure and relax the eyes. Then stop looking at anything, and relax the eyes further. Then, just let them go completely loose, not looking at anything, not doing anything, just resting the eyes—the loose, limp, relaxed eyes.

As you breathe freely, let the rest of your face be as relaxed as possible, looking at nothing, doing nothing, relaxing your eyes still more, and still more. Now, are the eyes relaxed more? Is your field of vision empty? Keep your eyes and your neck and your face as re-laxed as they can be, and then relax them still further. Observe the walking figure again. Are you able to see it without moving your eyes, with your eyes perfectly motionless and perfectly at rest? If you can still see that figure, then try to stop any movement remain-ing in your eyes, just letting go. Relax the eyes completely, and ob-serve whether that figure does not now disappear or fade away—if it had not already done so.

Continue to breathe freely and easily, and continue to let the eyes be just as relaxed as possible. At the same time, if there is any tension that has re-accumulated anyplace in your body that you are conscious of, now try to let go of that. Talk to that part of your body while you continue to relax and rest your eyes.

Now, let your eyes be as relaxed as possible. Do not look at anything. Let the tongue and throat relax as much as possible. Think about singing some popular song that you like. Sing it, but sing it without singing it aloud. Observe your tongue, and notice if you are aware of your tongue moving as you sing or of any movement in your throat or any changes in your neck. The idea is to try not to move your tongue as you sing and to remain relaxed in throat and neck. Try singing some hymn or other religious song that you knew as a child. Keep observing your tongue as you do it. Then try singing the national anthem. Observe the reactions in your tongue, your throat, your neck, around your mouth—release all tensions. Stop it a minute, and then try singing *America*. Observe what the tongue and mouth do. Notice if you can remember one of your early school songs. Not college, but earlier songs—high school, junior high, or elementary school—and sing that one. Finally, just sing something completely innocuous—a song you have no emotional involvement with—something you find pleasant, but innocuous.

Stop and let your tongue be as still and relaxed as possible, and also the jaw, mouth and throat. Now, just for a minute, think back to whether there were songs to which you responded especially strongly—as was evidenced by the tension that came into your tongue while you thought about singing it. What were the feelings that went with it? And what was the song? Now stick your tongue out vigorously several times, holding it for a few seconds as you did before. Then, each time, bringing it back, relaxing it completely, giving it all the time it might need to relax, and your mouth and throat as well. Do it several times until the relaxation seems as complete as possible. And let the rest of your body be very limp as well. Let your eyes relax just as much as possible and your whole body become as relaxed as it can be, including the neck, the throat, the mouth, the face, the eyes, the tongue. And just do nothing at all, just nothing at all.

No images, no ideas, no daydreaming, nothing. Just nothing.

Any time that you start to think, or your mind starts to wander, notice if there is any tension you can get rid of, and try again to fall back into that doing nothing—paying special attention when need be to relaxing the throat, the tongue and the eyes. The breathing should be free, easy, requiring no attention. And note whether now, as you do this lesson for the first time, you notice a diminishment in the flow of thought. Are you quieter in your mind than is your usual pattern? Do you notice that with that quiet comes a kind of serenity, a kind of quiet peace? You may, for at least a little while, have disrupted completely the usual inner chatter and imagery. In most cases, perhaps, the inner noise will be diminished but not eliminated altogether. But it will be significantly reduced so that you get a glimpse of what the more complete inner quiet could be.

It is important to get the glimpse—because when you do so, already you have disrupted the habitual way of functioning, weakened the tyranny of the unconscious, become a little more free, and more completely human—you have made a crack in the old pattern, and it is a crack that can now widen.

Practicing this exercise will, in time, help you to break the habitual flow through your head and mind of ideas and images. The more often you disrupt that flow—that chatter or noise, babble or cacophony, whatever it is—the easier it will be to achieve a normally more quiet mind. This will, in turn, augment the work you are doing to relax the muscles generally. You will find that as you are able to free your mind from that flow-through of ideas and images, you will also experience a corresponding decrease in emotions that come and go in you unbidden. You will be better able to self-regulate the flow of emotions.

And now, as you continue to lie there, observe again whether there remain some aftereffects of what you have just done. Is your mind still quieter than usual? If so, savor that quiet for a while, savor it a little while longer.

BRAIN FOCUSING TO HEIGHTEN SUGGESTIBILITY

Sit in a comfortable position, one that you will be able to maintain with minimal shifting. Close your eyes and direct your attention upward to the space where your brain is.

Almost everyone has some knowledge of what the brain looks like. Try to image or imagine it, particularly the two hemispheres of the brain. You know the brain has two hemispheres or sides to it. The two sides resemble each other for the most part.

On the surface, the brain looks as if it is covered with hills and valleys. The brain has convolutions and they look like a labyrinth you could roam.

Between those two hemispheres of your brain is what you might call a deep ravine or crevice that separates those two sides. This is called the *corpus callosum*, also sometimes referred to as the cerebral divide, which is a nice way of bringing together brain terminology and geographical language.

Think of those two hemispheres and the cerebral divide between them. As you try to image them, let your eyes roam around up in your brain space.

Let your eyes continue roaming, and observe just how clearly you can image the two hemispheres of your brain. Look down on it as though you were flying over some geographical feature of the earth, looking down on the hemispheres and the cerebral divide.

Feel that you are circling with your eyes at eye level so that you look around inside your head. Feel that you are looking at the back of it, then coming around and just making circles.

Try to create the *sensation* of circling just with the right eye in the space of the right hemisphere. Make vertical circles, circles that are slanted, as well as horizontal ones inside the space of the right hemisphere. Notice whether, as you do that, you feel movement in the left eye.

Concentrate on your right eye, but notice whether the left one moves, or if you feel it move. Is it possible to circle with one eye without circling with the other? In any case, what is the sensation?

Stop a moment and note whether you have a greater conscious-ness of the area of the right hemisphere than of the left. You may feel that the left side is empty. On the right side you may feel something where ordinarily you don't have sensation.

You might also feel that the whole right side of your face and head is more in your consciousness than the left side.

Return your attention to your brain space and feel yourself cir-cling with your left eye in the space of the left hemisphere.

Circle there horizontally, then vertically and at different an-gles.

Stop and note what this has done to your awareness. Are you now more aware of the left side, or are they now equal? Is there per-haps still more clarity to the feeling of something inside your skull?

Now circle a little above eye level, feeling that you are looking all around inside of your skull, and then circling higher. As you do that, move up from eye level, gradually making higher circles, the circles probably feeling somewhat smaller as you get near the top of your head.

Circle clockwise for a while, and then circle in the other direc-tion there in your brain space. Notice whether in the *whole* brain space you can make circles that tilt in one direction or the other. No-tice whether you can make vertical circles in different parts of your brain space. Can you make circles that seem to be just along the cere-bral divide, right between the hemispheres?

Experimenting with different kinds of circles within the brain space, be conscious just of that. To focus on a body part and to main-tain awareness of that part usually has the effect of improving the functioning of that part and also enables you to sense it better.

By any usual means, presumably, you cannot sense your brain.

Keep on making circles. This creates at least a feeling you are sensing your brain. Is there some other means of sensing that actually allows you to do it? Or what is it you will be sensing, because you clearly will have the feeling that something is there in that space as you continue making circles.

There is evidence which suggests that in fact you can improve brain functioning by doing this brain focusing. You can also do something else. This is a very good way of going into trance, including the self-induction of trance. For people who have trouble with autohypnosis, the continuing focus on the brain space will tend to result in an increase in suggestibility. The brain and the mind will become more suggestible, especially so with respect to altering the body and its functions. Therefore, if you want to effect bodily changes, the use of brain focusing as a means of heightening suggestibility is a particularly effective way.

Focusing mainly on the body seems to facilitate the acceptance of suggestions about the body, and focusing more on the mind would seem to facilitate the acceptance of suggestions about the mind and the emotions.

Continue to make circles a little above eye level and notice whether you circle spontaneously to the left or to the right.

In a moment, you will be told to stop this, but meanwhile continue to circle. When you are told to stop, you will stop right in the middle of your forehead above your nose someplace and then note how long you are able to keep the mind empty.

This is also a good way, in the beginning, to learn mind-emptying meditation. When the eyes stop circling, usually for almost anyone there will be at least some interval of time when the mind is empty of both words and images. For beginning meditators, that can be very difficult to achieve even momentarily.

Continue circling now, and in a moment when you are told to stop, just notice how long it takes before words and images come into your mind, or whatever else might come to break or interrupt that emptiness or stillness.

Circling and circling and circling in the brain space. Then when you get to the middle—*stop!*

Now, if something has intruded on that emptiness or stillness, just remark to yourself whether it was a word or an image or a physical sensation—whatever it was, just make a mental note of it— and then circle around again, just a little higher until you are told to stop again. Then you will let your mind remain empty, not thinking, not seeing, just quietly sensing the brain space and focusing on that point in front. Just continue circling.

Now stop! Notice whether you were aware of your breathing. If you have been aware of colors, notice what the colors were, if the colors are geometric or other forms, what the forms were like, whether words came into your mind or not. Were you aware of sounds? Were you aware of parts of your body that you were not focused on, and if so, was that awareness the same as it ordinarily is? Do you know what it ordinarily is? Is there any way it ordinarily is? Does it seem different?

Notice now whether the effort to empty the mind has diminished the feeling of something there inside the skull where the brain is. Is the seeming awareness of your brain greater or less than it was before you began emptying your mind? Make a lot of circles in the interior of your head with the intention of becoming increasingly aware of your brain. Just breathe easily and you can circle horizontally or at angles or vertically. You might also try just looking there, either looking in patterns or aimlessly, but with the intention of becoming increasingly aware of sensing something in that space.

Can you combine looking around in that brain space with the feeling of breathing into it and out of it?

With breathing, it is often possible to get several sensations in that space. As you breathe in and out, feel that the space there gets longer, stretches up, so to speak, elongates, then comes back down again with the exhalation. Feel that the head and the face can get longer and then shorter as you breathe—up and then down.

You can also very deliberately breathe through your two nostrils back toward your eyes, and beyond, with the intention of feeling that space widen and then get narrower. Notice if you can do that. That is, into the brain space so that it gets wider and then narrower. The brain feels as if it is pulsing—pulsating—expanding and contracting.

Observe now if it has become any easier to simultaneously breathe into the brain, or feel as if you are doing it, while you are moving your eyes around. When the eyes seem to roll around the brain space, then you can more easily make separate activities of the eye movements and the breathing.

Now stop. Sit very silently and notice what you are aware of in the brain space. Be aware with your eyes open. Notice if you can still remain as aware of your brain space or whether opening your eyes takes anything away. Now with the eyes open, breathe in so that the brain pulsates, expands and contracts as you breathe to the sides of your eyes, causing your head to seem to get wider and then narrower.

Close your eyes again. Ascertain if now it is easier to be truly aware of the brain as having two hemispheres. Can you really sense that there are two brains, two hemispheres? Notice the division between them. Not only can you sense something inside of your head, but you can get a sense that there are two hemispheres of the brain. Sense it more clearly than you could a moment ago before you opened your eyes.

Now think about the surface of the brain as convolutions, with hills and valleys on the surface. Imagine yourself in a small body and wandering around the labyrinth of your own convolutions. Wander around in the labyrinth of your brain and notice whether you begin wandering in the left hemisphere or the right. If you decide to cross over, how do you cross that cerebral divide? Do you go down into it, or weave from side to side, or fly or what? Just wander around in the convolutions a while. If you feel now that you are in trance or an altered state, just have the intention as you wander of going deeper in trance so you can *experience everything even more fully.*

Now descend into the cerebral divide where all the nerves are, standing over them or lying in that space. Note if you get any sense of nervous activity, whether it is like a humming, or whatever it might be. Can you get any sense of the chemical activity of your brain? The hemispheres are on either side of you and your consciousness is in the middle going up and down the divide, which is just lying in one place. Do you have any sense of movement? If so, what is it that moves and how many movements are there?

Determine what is in your field of awareness. As you breathe, notice if you breathe in such a way that not only does the brain pulsate but the two hemispheres move apart from each other a little bit so that the space in the cerebral divide widens and then gets narrower as you focus there and breathe. You feel that the hemispheres move in opposite directions, then back together again. Be certain that you do not hold your eyes rigid and thereby give yourself a headache.

Now do some circling again until told to stop. This time when told to stop, let your mind remain empty of all contents as long as you can. When it begins to fill in again, you will observe the sequence as well as the contents of the filling. But for now, just keep circling.

Reverse the circling a moment. Notice if it is becoming easier to reverse. Then revert to your original direction. Ascertain if you can circle as if the eyes were almost floating inside your head. Then, when you come to the middle of the forehead above the nose, *stop!*

Note if it is also possible to breathe so that it seems to you as you breathe in that the brain space extends behind you and as you breathe out that it extends in front of you, that it pushes forward and it pushes back. It might take you a minute to get the knack of it. Make it elongate and shorten, go out to the sides and back. You can also make it go backwards and forwards, and remark the sensations you have of your brain space as you do that breathing.

Now stop and note whether it seems to you that now your brain is breathing by itself without your directing breath towards it. Feel whether it is pulsating, or whatever it is that you are sensing in that space. Observe whether you can detect that. You may feel something almost like water lapping on the surface of a lake. Oceanic movement of pulsations.

Let your consciousness drift up and look down on your brain from above. Or otherwise get outside of it and see it more as a whole. Place your hands on the sides of your head and the top of your head so that the finger tips meet at the top. Continue breathing into that space and notice if your hands feel as if the head pulsates or expands and contracts a little.

When you can feel that, you are very close to actually holding your brain in your hands. The hand and the brain are reaching towards each other as though they both were trying to move through that thin shell that the skull has become so that they can make contact.

Now put your hands down, and focus on your brain space once more. Breathe into it a little, let your eyes roam around, bring it into the fullest possible awareness and increase the sensation there. You are very, very aware now of something in that space that ordinarily feels empty, very aware that there is something material lying in that space. Then using the next couple of minutes to speak directly to your brain, ask it to make changes for you that you desire and that the brain realistically can effect. Whether it is healing or changing certain bodily functions, perhaps changing habits or appetites, glandular activity or whatever it might be, talk to your brain directly and ask it to do these things.

Continue talking to your brain for another minute or two, and then in your own time open your eyes and take note of any perceptual changes in the room around you, the way you perceive people or objects. Then just gradually come up to a fresh, alert, waking state.

MEMORIES
AND PROJECTIONS

Lie on your back with your palms down at your sides. Scan your body. Lie flat on the floor and lie symmetrically. Note what you consider to be defects, or things that need to be changed. Try to arrange yourself in such a way that those asymmetries or misalignments or tension patterns, or whatever they are, are for the moment corrected. Such corrections do not help you to permanently change, but for the moment just do them anyway. Use whatever knowledge you think you have of how the body should lie and arrange yourself in that way, employing whatever means you find to do it.

Now roll to one side and sit up or do something to alter the arrangement just created. Then lie down again and observe the positions spontaneously "chosen."

Focus again on your body image, trying to have the clearest possible sense of how your entire body appears as you lie there; also sense how it feels. Now imagine its appearance and sensations when you are moving. Envision clothing it in various garments and also experience it without anything on. Have clear pictures and sensations of yourself so that you know just what your hands look like, what your feet look like, what your left shoulder looks like, your right ear, the middle of your back, your navel, your knees—every part of you.

Imagine yourself as a very tiny baby. Imagine what that body

155

would feel like. You probably have seen photographs that let you know what you looked like. Try to go into that baby's body and imagine what it is like to move around in it and all of the different movements that you make in that body. Try experiencing it even as a fetus, if you like.

Put special emphasis on the period when the body is learning to move in different ways, to creep and to crawl, to stand and to roll around. Actually do one movement with one foot and simultaneously another, different one with the other foot; begin to differentiate. Become aware of your mouth as not only a receptacle for food or thumb but also as an organ of speech and communication. Try to discern how many different movements you can make and how well you can imagine yourself in that tiny body.

Then advance to the age of five for a while. If you can, remember what that body was like, how it moved and what it did. If you cannot remember it, imagine it.

Then come up to about eight years and feel the difference; then ten years; then twelve. A twelve-year-old body may be very different from a ten-year-old.

Continuing, you can surely remember accurately, or fairly so, your fourteen-year-old body. Move around in that one for a while. Compare its strength and the way it moves with what you were doing at five or eight.

Come up to sixteen or seventeen and notice that there are more very major changes.

Then become twenty, and then twenty-five. If you are actually that age, project into the future as others recall a thirty-year-old body.

Sense how that body moves and how many different movements it makes and what kinds of movements. How many different movements does it make as compared to the baby or the ten-year-old or the fourteen- or fifteen-year-old?

Advance to a forty-year-old body, and then to one that is fifty. If you are looking into the future, rather than the present or past, create for yourself the body that realistically can be yours or is likely to be yours. Then go to sixty. Try to imagine the experience of a sixty-year-old body and how you want yours to be. Then go to a seventy-year-old body, and then as many more years as your destiny might give you, perhaps age seventy-five or eighty or even older.

It is possible for you, if you are willing to make the effort, to have practically any kind of body that you want, within the limits of whatever is possible by straightening the skeleton and increasing the spaces between the joints to increase your height. You can sculpt your body and make it pretty much whatever you would like it to be, especially a decade from now, assuming that you are alive then and have no serious illnesses or accidents. It can be and feel almost any way that you would like to make it. It is just a question of motivation.

Project yourself ten years into the future and assume that you have used yourself well. See yourself having gained, if you do not have it now, good knowledge about nutrition and having abandoned those practices that are seriously detrimental to your health.

Imagine that you have brought your weight to a proper level and done cardiovascular exercises for fitness, as well as a great deal of psychophysical work, so that your body is able to move very well and you also sense it with great clarity. You waste very little energy with the result that you do not get tired; you are able to self-regulate it to a very high degree so that the body is made extremely sensitive. The senses are all very, very alive.The body image is sharp. Your awareness is extremely keen. You have established for yourself a condition of optimal health relative to the ordinary person. You have done what is well within your means, if you are motivated to do it.

Try to sense and imagine as clearly as you can that body which you are going to have ten, or even twenty, years from now.What is it going to feel like? How is it going to move? What is it going to look like? Will it necessarily look any older? In the case of older people, could it even look younger? The older you are, the more likely that it can look younger.

When you have projected the image of the body you would like to have and which can realistically be yours barring some unforeseeable obstacle, then place that body and personality that goes with it into a number of different situations and observe it. Determine if it is satisfactory or if there is something about it you want to change.

Then inquire also what you have done during those years and what you wish you had done so that should you choose to create a plan of growth and enrichment, you could be helped by looking back now from a projection of yourself into the future. Consider what you wish you had done or not done with your life in the ten or twenty years between the projection and the present time. What kind of person can you realistically be if you set out to achieve your goals now? What can you have done in ten years? What kinds of powers can you possess? What will you have done in the world that you will feel will have been worthwhile? For what do you want to be remembered?

When you make the projection of the body image, add onto it those accomplishments as if you had already achieved them. Be certain they are things that you realistically believe you can do and would like to do. When you have projected that image, which includes growth and accomplishment, hold that image strongly for a little while.

It is a law of human life that images can be concretized. If you hold them long and vividly enough, they tend to become reality; they are self-fulfilling prophecies. Realities are born out of an image or a constellation of images.

If you were to do a sufficiently careful analysis of your past, you would almost certainly find that in many ways you are now the actualization and potentiation of past images, images that you had of yourself and, in some cases, images that you allowed other people to impose on you.

Those who will be parents should understand that the imposing of images on others also imposes a very heavy burden on those others. Most parents do not know their children at all and do not love their children at all. They love images they have of the child. As the child increasingly diverges from the image, it is increasingly the image, rather than the child, that the parent is involved with. While you do not forsake your task of giving guidance and help, you have to give an unconditional love that allows the child to be what he or she is and not expect the child to live according to *your* image of what *you want* him or her to be or what *you think* that he or she is.

Almost every one of you will find, if you look for it enough, that you have in some ways fulfilled the image that your parents had of you. If that image is in you, then you have to decide whether or not to undertake the task of eliminating the image in order to really become yourself. This means separating the *personality* from *essence* and then making appropriate changes, difficult as that is to do.

If by now you have left it, go back to that image of what you could be and want to be. Concentrate on it very, very vividly and intend that you will move toward it.

As long as you hold some very clear image of what you want to be, an image that incorporates your physical, mental, emotional and spiritual being, that you can move towards, then your life is much less likely to drift or be buffeted by circumstance. You have a much better chance of realizing a larger part of your potential. The image is an immensely powerful tool for moving towards that end of becoming what you want to be.

The physical aspect of that image is extremely important because it grounds the other components of the image in something very, very concrete. The physical self is easy, comparatively speaking, to image, and it also provides a foundation of probable health and physical effectiveness that is usually essential if you are going to do the other things.

Concentrate on the image for several minutes and make it as completely what you want as possible. Take several minutes to do that. Those minutes can seem like a very long time to you subjectively to the extent that you immerse yourself in the world of the image. Just relax and know that as you do the psychophysical and psychospiritual work you become better and better able to shape the future, your own future, if you avail yourself of the powerful images that you are being taught how to make.

JOURNEY INWARD

Lie on your back and think about the joints of your body, beginning with your toes and your ankles. Think of those joints of which you are conscious, which you feel, and also think of major joints of which you may not be aware, such as the spinal vertebrae. As you go over your body, suggest to yourself that the relevant muscles are relaxing, becoming longer and looser, so that the joints can release.

Now pay attention to your eyes and to your breathing. If your eyes are open, close them and leave them closed. Note how your breathing affects your eyes, how they rise and fall with your breathing, and whatever else you can notice. Begin to notice that when you exhale the eyelids get heavier and the eyes close tighter. Let the eyes close tighter with each exhalation, but only the eyes, without tightening any of the muscles of your face. Your strong focus on breathing and on the sensations around your eyes will continue to affect you by altering your consciousness, deepening your state, even though you no longer focus on the breathing or on the eyes, as we begin our *Journey Inward*—rather as we *continue* it, for it already has begun.

Focus again on your breathing and, as you exhale, go deeper and feel your eyelids closing a little tighter each time. Exhaling— now, as you continue to do that, be aware of the top of your head, your skull, around your brain space.

161

Be aware of the top and the back of your skull and of the sockets of your eyes. Be aware of your jaw, your jawbone, your teeth, and of the spine, the neck and bones of the neck coming up into the skull, and then your spine all the way down your body.

Be aware of the shoulder girdle, the shoulder joints, the ribs, the upper and lower arms, the hands. Become increasingly aware of your skeleton—pelvic bones, hip joints, upper legs, lower legs, and feet. Go deeper in and think of yourself as just a skeleton lying there, just bones.

And then begin to add on some of the muscles and organs of the body so that it is a body with no facade, no skin on the outside, a body like you see in anatomical charts and anatomy books with just the inside present, and just part of that available to you. And then feel something of what you are like without your facade, without that surface which presents your image to the world.

Add the blood flowing, the body's chemistry, electrical activity, and connections between the brain and the parts of the body through the nervous system. Gradually let the body acquire a skin, a surface, and be aware of the surface and of what is inside. Then, directing your attention inward from the surface, pass into your body at any point and *explore* inside—*exploring* wherever you like and observing the activity in different parts of your body.

Explore inside one of your hands and then travel up that arm, that shoulder, and pass into your chest, observing your breathing, the lungs, air coming into and then out of them as you breathe. Continue *exploring* and pass up through your throat and into your head, *observing* your brain, and moving into and through the brain.

Begin to explore at more and more microscopic levels. First, go into the bloodstream, flowing with the blood and becoming aware of the blood all around in that one part of your body. Have an increasingly microscopic kind of awareness so that a tiny drop of blood can be all around you. And you can penetrate skin tissues and be able to go into bones. Microscopic awareness—tiniest parts—until finally you will become aware even of atoms and molecules and going beyond that to even subatomic levels of yourself. Observe yourself as particles in movement. Even though from the outside and from your own experience your body seems to be more or less stable, experience it as billions of particles in movement, held together by no one is quite certain what.

Continue to roam within at the minutest levels of your physical reality you can penetrate. Observe colors, sounds, sensations, and if you can find them, smells and tastes. Then, from whatever part of your body you are in, return to the brain. If you are not there already, return to your brain.

Now, as you have explored your body, you can explore your mind. As you went deeper and deeper into your bodily reality, conceive of your mind as having levels and go deeper and deeper down through those levels of mind. Observe what you find there, and what the inscape of the mind looks like as compared to that of the body. Are they the same? Are the mind and the body one? Or are they separate?

As you keep going in deeper, if you discover *where to look,* you can find in the mind whatever you found in the body. But can you also find in the body whatever you find in the mind? You can explore them as one reality or as two, without making any definitive statement about whether it is one reality or two. Observe whether you experience mind and body as separate realities or as a single reality.

You will now take several minutes of clock time. If your mental processes accelerate, that can be a very, very, long time subjectively, experientially, for exploring the realities of mind and body—or perhaps what you experience as the single reality of body/mind. Explore now one or both, whatever you like, suggesting to yourself that your mental processes *will* accelerate so that those several minutes can include as much experience as you would ordinarily have in a much, much longer time period.

Now, as you explore and experience, ask yourself whether one appears to be illusory. Is the mind real or an illusion? Is the body real or an illusion? Might they both be real, or might they both be illusions?

So far we have made a two-part division into body and mind—at least for the purposes of exploration. Now we consider that one might make a three-part division and say that existence is not only bodily and mental, but also spiritual. Existence includes a person's body and mind and spirit—that there is a *bodily* reality *to be experienced,* a *mental* reality *to be experienced,* and a *spiritual* reality *to be experienced.* You have gone into your own body. You have gone into your own mind. Now, go into your own spiritual dimension and observe whether that is the same as the mind or something different. Or the same as the body or something different? Whether all three are one, or whether there is some other way of looking at it? For the next several minutes, then, go as deeply and as far as you can into your own *spiritual reality.*

Then observe whether you can pass beyond that into something that is beyond any self—not anyone's body or anyone's mind or anyone's spirit. Observe dimensions that are beyond any particular existence—transpersonal, cosmic, whatever one might choose to call that—and find the atmosphere around you increasingly holding a sense of great power; enter a place of very great power, but a power that is *tranquil* and *serene. A very, very powerful force* without any hint of menace or negation, a *completely positive serene kind of power.* Just remain in that space and allow that extremely positive serene power to permeate you, your spirit, your mind, your body, your whole self, partaking of it and being filled with it. You can have a very long experience of that for the next few minutes of clock time.

Then, with that powerful, benevolent life force in you, and its serenity filling you so that you are like a glowing body of white light as you move, make your way back through the cosmic transpersonal realm into your own spiritual world, through your own mind and through your own body, back up to the surface. You have several minutes of clock time during which you can completely or very fully experience all those realms as you come back through the same regions you passed in arriving at the place where you are. *Begin that journey now.*

Know that by passing through these different grounds you further *unify yourself.* You help to make yourself *more whole* so that within your being the orchestration and the *integration* of the whole proceeds better, with freer access and more profound levels, with some of the *obstructions eliminated* as you move towards *self-fulfillment,* larger humanity, much *greater realization of your potentials.*

Count, now, for yourself, from twenty to one. You are emerging from the trance, stretching, bringing back with you your experiences and any feelings you want to bring back—images, ideas, understandings—whatever you want to bring back, bring. Do that, counting yourself out of the trance. Do it until you are awake—stretching, enjoying feeling your body and the rest of you, then sitting up, and being prepared for life in the external world.

GIANT LUMINOUS BODY

Seat yourself on the floor in a yoga-type position, or some other position you can easily sustain for a while, and close your eyes. This exercise is a variation on an ancient Tibetan and also Egyptian practice which, in most cases, will lead spontaneously to altered states of consciousness.

Close your eyes and be aware of yourself sitting there as I speak. Think of a seated figure with a human body but the head of a lion or lioness in an altered state of consciousness or trance. Your consciousness can alter to any degree during the course of this exercise. It can alter a little or it can alter profoundly. It will not require any effort of any kind on your part or even awareness that it is happening. It is in the nature of the exercise itself that the consciousness will alter.

Now, as you sit there, identify for a moment with that seated God- or Goddess-like figure, and be aware especially of the feeling around the top of your head where your brain is. Be aware of your third eye region. Be aware of the base of your brain. Be aware of the top of your head. Be aware of your spine, all the way down and up. Be aware of your throat, your heart region, your solar plexus, your center. Be aware of the entire pelvis and especially of the base of the spine.

Bring the awareness up the spine to the head and to the brain.

Now, think of yourself and feel yourself as you sit there growing larger and larger and larger. You will have to be sitting in an imagined space that will allow you to expand in all directions. Note that seated in this position your form is much like that of a pyramid, growing wider and taller until your form is gigantic.

Experience standing up in that gigantic form and continue to grow larger and larger and larger until your form leaves the atmosphere of the earth somewhere down around your feet, and your awareness is of space—your form is becoming so gigantic that you can reach out and hold a star or planet in your hand, having it rest in the palm of your hand—and you are able to run across the heavens, running with great strides out and out into the far reaches of space, with a whole infinity to run in.

You find out there animals with immense zodiacal signs, animals made of stars that you can ride, a great horse or a lion or a goat, many kinds of beasts that you can ride through the heavens. You find yourself for a moment with a bow and an arrow as you assume the identity of an archer, drawing back the bow and letting the arrow go out and out and out forever into space.

You are just drifting in space, alone again, not having to run or to ride, drifting in space, a great cosmic figure with arms out and legs spread. Observe yourself going farther and farther out into the vastness of space. Then, you are conscious that even as these things have happened, your feet have remained on the earth and that you stand on the earth, a giant figure, that your form is translucent and that energy like stars flows up and down through that translucence, and also flows in color—all kinds of colors, and glittering stars and particles of energy flowing through the body so that they can be seen from the outside. You can stand outside your body with your consciousness or just know what is happening inside of it.

Far, far down you can observe the color flowing through your legs. And look for the subtle body organs and centers, the color and the light and the energy flowing into each one on up to your head. See what this body has inside of it, where those centers are. Does it have anything like a skeleton, muscles? Does it have a spine, a heart?

Be aware of your body standing and of its freedom from the constraints of nature as you know it. You can extend your right arm and let it grow longer and longer and longer until it extends even beyond the reach of your own vision—and the other arm as well.

The feet can go down through the earth—the legs getting longer and longer—until you stand on the earth's very center and your arms can wrap around the earth until your hands meet and clasp and you hold the earth in your embrace.

Then, by another metamorphosis you stand again on the earth with your arms and legs as they were before, an immense translucent body of light, observing again the beautiful colors flowing through it, the dance of energy. See if you can observe the life itself pulsing, flowing within that body. Then raise your awareness up through your throat to the inside of your head, a head that is expanding and expanding, so that you can see better and better a larger and larger picture of what is going on inside the brain and other parts of your head—the head of that giant figure of light who is yourself.

Now, for a little while feel the power of this immense body, the strength. Let tempests hurl themselves against it, and bolts of lightning and great tidal waves. Experience how this body delights in its strength, and how it can laugh at the elements. Not earth, nor water, nor air, nor fire can harm it. Feel that this body has the power to ascend into the sky—wants to go up and up and up.

It can descend and walk across the floor of the ocean and in the waters. It can rise out of the waters and walk through the solid rock of mountains. It can pass through regions of fire. It can float over the abyss—the bottomless void—without any fear of falling.

Now, standing in your giant luminous body of light, try to feel it and know it as completely as you can. Lie down and experience it. Experience it as you sit in the position of a magician-priest or -priestess or a yogi. Perceive this body of light to be a body fully realized by a SÂHU priest or some similar enlightened and realized being.

As you sit in that position and that body, realize that it also is a great temple, its architecture both complex and beautiful. Wander around inside of it, experiencing that, seated. The body is a structure you can go into. Then observe that you are seated on this floor and you are your everyday corporeal body, the same size as it usually is. Then, sense it and compare it with the body of light—the immense luminous body.

CREATING AND EXPERIENCING
AN IMAGINAL BODY
AND ITS TRANSFORMATIONS

This exercise is to be done seated in a comfortable straight-backed armless chair, one you do not sink into too much. For optimal results, the exercise should take approximately two hours and could take even longer. Allow ample time for each experience described until the crucial timing has been mastered. Remember, imaged movements should be repeated about 25 times as actual physical movements are done in typical psychophysical re-education exercises.

In previous exercises you have used images of movement to bring about changes in your body. Those have mostly been movements imagined or imaged with respect to the actual physical body. There is another way of effecting changes that is less well known and that should be a part of any authentic spiritual discipline or Work of an esoteric School. That way is to perform the movements with a body that is also a product of the imagination, to create a second body that is an imaginal body and to move that one. You then observe the effects of the movement of that body on the physical body.

Now make yourself comfortable with your feet resting on the floor. Imagine that you are sitting opposite yourself, facing yourself. The experience of this ranges all the way from just having a faint notion of what it would look like to being able to see oneself as clearly as if one were actually there in both places. Now try for a moment to imagine the consciousness that is used or that manifests in out-of-body experiences—for instance, when someone has had an accident and the consciousness looks down at the body as it is lying there on the ground. Try to shift your consciousness so that you look down at your physical body sitting in the chair. Discover how well you are able to know what it looks like.

Then imagine yourself in the form in which we are going to work, and that is lying down somewhere in front of yourself. Imagine yourself on your back, your hands at your sides. Your hands and arms are at your sides and your palms are down. Your feet are separated by 12 or 13 inches. Turn the right foot to its outside. For now, only move the right foot of the imaginal body. With that imaginal body, turn the foot onto its right side by rotating your right hip out, and then bring it back to the middle. Repeat that imagined movement about 25 times. Bring the outside of the right foot as close to the floor as you can and then bring it back. Be aware of the outside of the foot as it touches the ground. Then stop.

Now just flex and extend the toes of the right foot of your imaginal body. Flex and extend the toes and experience that sensation. Then flex and extend the ankle a few times. Feel just as clearly as you can what that body is feeling. Do not imagine that the body sitting in the chair is doing anything. The sensations are all with regard to the body that is lying there before you.

Make some circles with your right foot by rotating the ankle. Make some in one direction for a while, and then circle in the other direction. Remember, all these movements are performed by your imaginal body only.

Then bend both legs of that imaginal body so that your feet are standing on the floor. Rap with the ball of your right foot on the floor. Do it rather vigorously. See where you have to place your foot so as to do it. Then rap with the heel and you will see that you have to bring your foot into a different relation to your bottom in order to rap well with your heel. Where you rap best with the ball of your foot is not where you rap best with your heel.

Then just pick the foot up and put it down a number of times on its bottom. Keep the leg bent and just raise the foot and put it down.

Let your right leg stand alongside your left one. Let it fall over to your right side, approaching the floor as closely as it will, and bring it back. Keep doing that. Be aware of the movement in the hip joint and the arc that your right knee makes through space as it goes over to one side and then comes back to the middle. Then stop.

Pick your right foot up and make circles with the right knee in the air. Circle in one direction and then in the other. Then stop.

Bring your right leg back towards you so that the top of your right thigh approaches your rib cage. Be certain that what you feel are the sensations of the imaginal body and that you are doing everything with reference to that body, which is lying on the floor. Now stop.

Leave the right arm on the floor and rap with the right hand, bending at the wrist. Be aware not only of the bending of your wrist and of the rapping of your hand but of the sound that your hand makes when rapping on the floor. Then continue rapping with your hand on the floor, but do it by picking up your entire arm. Keep your arm extended, elbow straight. Raise it several inches off the floor and bring the hand down so that you can make even louder rapping. Then stop.

Slide your right hand up and down along the floor by pushing and pulling from the right shoulder. Feel the floor beneath the hand and the arm. Now instead of listening to the rapping, you are using your tactile sense to feel the floor. You are using your kinesthetic sense to feel the movement in the shoulder and the movement of the hand and the arm. You also use your visual sense as you look at the body and observe the hand moving up and down. For a moment, you make your consciousness dual. You feel the body moving as you identify with it and you also detach yourself from it and look at it. You can see it moving. You can see and feel the movement simultaneously. You get as completely as possible into your imaginal body.

Put your right arm out to your side at shoulder height. Bend the arm at the elbow. Make many circles with the hand and the arm, rotating at the elbow. Make a number of circles in one direction and a number of circles in the other direction. Make small ones and big ones, quick ones and slow ones. Be certain to feel what is happening in the elbow and the movement of the hand and the arm through space. Then stop.

Put your right hand over the right side of your chest. Let the palm rest on your chest on the right side. Raise and lower the elbow towards the ceiling, like the flapping of a wing. Raise your elbow as high as you can towards the ceiling, and then bring it back down against the floor. See how quickly and lightly you can make that movement.

Then finally, instead of raising the elbow towards the ceiling, flap the elbow towards your hip, with your hand remaining on your chest so that your arm comes down against your rib cage. Then raise the elbow to shoulder height and continue flapping in this manner approximately 25 times. Then extend the arm again.

Lie still on the floor and scan your imaginal body. Determine whether you feel that the two sides are the same, or whether one side feels longer, or one side tilts more, or one side is clearer. Ascertain what you can feel. You have only imagined moving an imaginary body, and you have not imagined any movement for your actual physical body. Turn your attention now to your physical body and observe what you feel. Note if there is any difference in the clarity of the right and left sides of the actual physical body. Compare your right eye with your left eye, your right hand with your left, your right knee and foot with your left knee and foot.

Now get up and move around with your actual physical body. Walk around and determine what else you notice. If now the right side feels different from the left side, try to carefully note what the differences are on the two sides. Also compare this to what you feel when you do imaginary work with the physical body. Remark whether you can discriminate any difference between the change that occurs by working on the imaginal body with images or imagination and working on the physical body with images or imagination.

Notice if you can feel that your body now on the right side has a different kind of energy feeling than when you work on the physical body. Try to define for yourself what the difference is. Note whether the awareness of the left side is more or less than when you work on the physical body, either actually or with imagination.

You can understand from this, at the very least, how the experience of the body in dreams, which is an experience of an imaginal body and not a physical one, affects the experience of the physical body. You see a demonstration of it right now here in yourself that what happens to the imaginal body changes the physical body. This is much closer to the dream experience or to the kind of experience that is taught in Shamanism or the spiritual disciplines.

In a dream, you have no sense of *imaging* that something is happening. With the dream body, almost always you have an actual body that things happen to and that you use. The only difference between that and what you are doing here is that here the consciousness is detached and one part is looking at another part so that you have two bodies. Eventually, you can place your consciousness in the imaginal or kinesthetic body to such an extent that the physical body will be lost altogether. You will have no awareness of yourself as a person sitting in a chair. The only reality you will know is the body lying on the floor. You may even achieve that here. Now come back and sit in your chair.

Make yourself comfortable. Close your eyes and breathe right up the middle of your body, up what we call the "core line," as if there is a line that runs from between your legs right up to the top of your head. Breathe up and down that line right along the middle of your body as if the breath is coming in through your bottom and coming out through the top of your head, and then back down, in and out. When the feeling is well established that your breath is moving up and down your center, imagine your second body, another body, lying before you on its back. While you are doing that breathing in your physical body, try to do the same thing with your imaginal body. Actually feel it in your imaginal body as you felt the movements when you were doing all the movements on your right side. It is usually very, very difficult at first to do a movement with the imaginal body while also physically doing the same, or an opposing movement.

Bend the legs of your imaginal body so the feet are standing. Let the right leg of the imaginal body drop over, and bring it back, and keep doing that. At the same time, take the left leg of the physical body over to the side and bring it back. See if you can do both of those things together, without sacrificing the awareness of the imaginal body. Now stop.

Scan your physical body as you sit there. Note whether your right side is still clearer than your left. Are you symmetrical now? As you remain seated, let your imaginal body get up and walk around. It does not have to walk around this room. It can walk around any space you like. Feel its movement. Occasionally, look at it from the outside so you see yourself, as in an out-of-body experience. See the imaginal body rather than the physical body. Note if, when you look at it from the outside like that, the imaginal body is also using its eyes—if you can see out of two bodies at one time or whether, when you look at the imaginal body from the outside, it has no experience of seeing.

Then go back into your imaginal body and walk around with it as it looks at its environment. Then move it into a different environment in an entirely different place. Move around there. Now put it successively in two or three other different environments. Explore moving around in them, looking and listening, smelling and tasting. Experience each place as fully as you can. Try being aware of every sensation—the contact of the foot with the ground, how the ankles bend, the knees, the hip joints, the hands, the elbows, the shoulders, how you carry yourself, how you breathe. Be as completely aware of both yourself and the environment as you can be. It is as if you are doing a mindfulness exercise, but doing it now in the imaginal body. Now stop.

Get up with your physical body and stretch just a minute. Wake yourself up and become alert.

Now sit down and make yourself comfortable. Close your eyes and then once again place the imaginal body on the floor in front of you where you worked on it before, legs and arms extended. This time you will do some work for a while on your left side. You will do quickly some of the things that were done in a bit more elaborate fashion on the right side.

First, take the left leg of your imaginal body over to the outside, rotating your hip so that the outside of the foot approaches or touches the floor. Then bring it back and continue rotating your left hip joint. And stop.

Now flex and extend the toes of the left foot. Sense very clearly what you are doing.

Now flex and extend the left ankle. You can do it in such a way that you rock your body along the floor, or you do not need to do that. If you do decide to rock your body, note that when the foot comes back, the chin moves away from the chest. When the foot goes down, the chin comes down towards the chest and the shoulder also moves. Then stop.

Bend both legs of your imaginal body and place your feet on the floor. Rap with your left heel. Place the foot at that distance from the body that allows you to rap most easily with your left heel. Note whether if you put your foot too close to your body or too far away it is impossible for you, even in your imagination and in an imaginal body, to rap with your left heel. It is bound by the same laws in such a matter as is the physical body. Place the foot so that you can rap easily with the ball of the foot. Do that a few times and then stop.

Let your left leg drop over to the side. Bring it back to the middle and continue to let it go as far left as it will. Extend your right leg as you do that. As you take the left leg over to the left and bring it back, let it come over the right until it lies on the right leg and goes past it. Then increase the movement from left to right with the left leg by moving the extended right leg out of the way. Now stop.

Again bend the right leg of the imaginal body so that both feet are standing on the floor. Rap on the floor with your left hand just by bending your wrist. The rest of the left arm remains on the floor. Listen to the rapping. Then make it louder by raising the entire arm and slapping with the hand on the floor.

Let your left arm rest at your side like the right one. Just make some circles with the left on the floor. The palm of the hand inscribes circles, going in one direction and then in the other. Do some clockwise and some counterclockwise. Try doing it without bending the elbow so that it is entirely a shoulder movement. Then allow the elbow to bend so that it is mainly an elbow movement. Then extend your left arm again and let it lie at your side.

Slide your left hand up and down along the floor, sensing movement in the shoulder. At the same time, use your tactile sense and feel the surface of the floor beneath your hand. Determine if you can make a more refined discrimination so that part of the time you are trying to learn mainly about the floor and part of the time you are trying to learn mainly about what your hand is feeling. Shift back and forth between the self and the not-self with the imaginal body and the imaginal sensory apparatus.

Then place your left hand on your chest, with your arm out at approximately shoulder height. Raise your elbow towards the ceiling, flapping your arm like the wing of a bird. Flap it up and down. Then put your right hand also on your chest and do the same movement so that both arms are flapping up and down. As you do that, think of a bird flapping its wings. Then, as you continue to do that, discover that in fact your body is the body of a bird. Look at it from the outside as a great bird soaring from the heavens, flapping its wings. Feel the wings flapping and the body of the bird soaring in the sky. Remark what else you can feel. Be aware of what kind of bird it is and what it looks like. Enjoy the feeling of the flapping wings and the body soaring in the sky, looking down at the land beneath you. See the water, or whatever else is there. Sometimes let the wings just be extended and floating along in the sky. Enjoy that experience for a while, flying. Then cease movement.

Let your consciousness hang suspended and without form until you find yourself in the body of a large cat, a tiger, a lion, whatever you feel yourself into. Be aware of moving now in that body—the power of it, the grace of it, whatever else you feel. It has four legs, a huge and powerful body, and yet it is moving so lightly. Note what that consciousness feels like and what you see looking out of the eyes. Compare it with the experience of being a bird, with the bird's consciousness.

Leave that body and let your consciousness hang suspended. Then find yourself in the body of a great serpent, a snake. Feel that body as it undulates and slithers along the earth with its tongue darting in and out of its mouth. How does it sense the earth? What does it see when you look out through its eyes? What does its consciousness feel like? Compare it with being a great cat and a bird.

Then, with your consciousness hanging suspended once again, find yourself in the body of an elephant. Feel that enormously massive body with the small brain high up off the ground. What does it feel like to move? What does the earth feel like beneath its giant feet? How does the world look to that being?

Then find your consciousness transferred instead to the body of a whale, and then a dolphin, or whatever other sea creature you like. Sense it moving and leaping through the water. What do you hear and see? What is your experience? How does the large dolphin brain differentiate its experience from the others?

Then, once again find yourself back in the body of a bird flying high over the place where the elephant, the great cat, the serpent and the other creatures are, as well as over the sea where the sea animals and fish are. Enjoy the feeling of the wings both flapping and gliding. Stop flapping the wings and just glide now. Find that as you glide, you glide no longer in the body of a bird but in your own human form. You now can fly. You can move your arms like the flapping of a bird's wings and find that your arms will carry you through the sky. Shamans fly. Flapping your wings or gliding with your arms extended, look down at the ground and you can see the shadow that you cast, like a strange cross passing over.

Now observe if by yourself you can assume several other different forms. Transform your imaginal body but experience the sensations of whatever you decide to become. Sense the movements and the sensations, and also the perceptions and emotions. Identify with those beings as completely as possible.

Now place your imaginal body on the floor again, and let it rest there. Then bring your consciousness back into your physical body seated in the chair. Let the imaginal body rise up out of that consciousness and walk around the room where you are. Sense its movements very, very clearly; sense its sensations and the environment. Notice if it has become any easier to move into the imaginal body and to experience with it. Also, use it to do things like running and leaping, lying down and rolling, rolling and rolling over grassy surfaces, whirling like a dervish. Let it be agile and free. Pay attention to its feelings and sensations because that makes it easier and easier to be in it. Use it and feel what it feels. Give it interesting, pleasurable experiences. That reinforces the creative processes that produced the imaginal body. It creates a desire to go into it. Such experiences strengthen it.

Now just come back to your own body sitting in the chair. Let the imaginal body merge with it, drawing back into it until there is no distinction between the two that you experience at all. Nothing of it is left outside of yourself.

Close your eyes. Sense clearly your own body, your physical, everyday body. Then open your eyes. Move around and feel more and more alert and also very, very relaxed. Get up and move around. Become wider and wider awake as you move.

MAKING THE BODY
WITH TWELVE ARMS

To begin with, walk around for a while and observe your movements. Pay particular attention to the movements in your shoulders. Do not walk in any special way; just walk in the way that you ordinarily walk when you are not self-observing. When studying behavior, there is not only an "observer effect" but there is also a "self-observer effect" to take into account.

As you continue moving, raise both arms to shoulder height. Now raise them to shoulder height the *other* way. That is, if you raised them initially to the sides, now raise them to the front. If you raised them to the front, now raise them to the sides. Take your arms down and keep on raising and lowering them, alternating between the two ways of raising your arms to shoulder height. Stop and rest.

Now, raise your arms overhead towards the ceiling and lower them, repeating those movements for a while. Then make circles with both arms, taking them forward and down, then backward and up, as you make those big circles. Try doing just one arm at a time, alternating the movements of the two arms, and notice if that makes the circling easier.

Note whether these movements feel smooth and unimpeded to you, or whether it seems to you that there is some obstruction, that your shoulder joints do not rotate as freely as they ought to. Do a number of circles with one arm, then a number of circles with the other arm. Compare the movements of the two arms and shoulders—does one move better, or are they about the same? If there is a difference, remember it. Have the intention of remembering in detail all the movements you have done until now—the sensations, the freedom, or lack of it, whatever you have noticed. You will want to be able to compare that with the movements and sensations you will experience later on. Now just lie down on your back.

Sense your shoulders in relation to the floor. Try to sense your spine in your neck. Sense the top of it and try to follow it down all the way to the base of the spine. Note if it seems to you that your spine is straight or if you can get any sense of it at all that would let you know if it is straight or not. Try positioning your body so that your spine feels straight, regardless of what your mind tells you about whether that position is correct or not. Go on just the basis of feeling.

Then, breathe as if by breathing you could breathe right along the line where you sense your spine to be. Notice if the breathing makes your spine seem to be straighter or if you have difficulty feeling that you can breathe along a straight line which also coincides with your spine. In some cases you will find that you breathe more to one side of the spine than it seems that you should. If that is so, notice whether the other nostril is not a little clogged, explaining why the breathing is off to one side.

If you feel that you are breathing to one side, put your finger alongside the nostril on that side and see if the other one is not breathing as freely. Check to find out if you are breathing equally through both. Put your finger alongside one nostril and close it for a moment and then do it with the other one. Note if your breathing is what you sensed it to be.

Now bend your legs and let your feet rest on the floor in a comfortable position, one that allows the lumbar spine to come as close to the floor as possible. Again, note if you can get a sense of your spine. You can start at the bottom or the top. If you need to raise your pelvis a few times to put your lumbar spine on the floor, do that.

Bring your legs back towards your chest and rib cage, and take hold of your knees with your hands. Pull the legs towards you and release them, keeping the hands on the knees. Do it so as to maintain the maximum contact of the small of your back with the floor. Continue bringing your knees lightly towards you and let them fall away. Now do so alternately, bringing first one knee and then the other towards the chest. Make smooth, continuous movements. Pay attention to the contact of the small of your back with the floor. Then release your knees.

Leave your feet and legs off the floor, with your knees touching. Take your feet and legs side to side, carefully, swiveling from your pelvis. Remember not to move too strenuously. Let them just go back and forth easily.

Cross your legs. Take hold of one foot with each hand. Bring the knees toward you and take them away. Hold onto the toes with your fingers, the toes and the tops of your feet. Just keep bringing them towards you.

Now, without releasing your feet, put the leg that is on top underneath. Then put it back again. Now you see that both hands are on the outside. Both arms are on the outside of the legs. Reverse them again so that the other leg is on top and one arm is now inside of your legs and one is outside. In the case of the foot that feels that you have the less comfortable hold on, let go of it for a minute and take hold of it from the other side with your hand. See if that feels better.

Rock back and forth a little. Pull your knees towards your chest and take them away. Your heels should be close to your bottom, if not resting against it. Pull your knees back towards your chest. Reverse the position of your legs again. Just take them back and forth a few times, going from one position to the other. Also, when the position of the legs changes, put your hand in the most comfortable position on your foot. Do you remember whether initially your right foot or your left foot was on top?

Put your feet down in a standing position. Without thinking, pick them up and cross your legs again and notice which one goes on top, the left or the right. Then if you have the left one on top, put the right one on top, and keep switching back and forth.

Take hold of your feet with your hands and bring your knees back towards you, and let them go away. All the time, feel the contact of your back with the floor. Reverse the position a number of times, keeping hold of the feet with the hands, one leg inside an arm and one arm inside a leg. Try to do it lightly and easily. Determine how quickly you can switch back and forth. Then stop and rest with your legs extended on the floor.

Now bend your legs and let your feet stand on the floor. Let your right leg go over to the side. Keep your feet on the floor and let your right leg drop over to your right side. Sense the movement in the small of your back. Continue to do it. Sense on up your back, and as you sense higher, notice if you feel the rib cage as it moves to the right and makes a different contact with the floor. Let your right leg go all the way over as it will. Try letting your head turn with your leg.

Then, instead of going right, go left with the left leg. Note whether the head goes with it or if you have to move the head by an effort of will. Pay attention especially to the contact of your back with the floor. Then stop.

Try once again to sense your spine. Place yourself so that it seems that your spine is straight. Even though you might know from an intellectual point of view that your body is crooked, arrange it so that it feels that the spine is straight. Go on feeling, even though you might think you know that what you are doing is wrong.

Now push and pull with your feet to rock your body along the middle of the spine. Try to push in such a way that the spine moves up and down right through the middle and you are not leaning more on one side or the other. It is a perfect movement up and down along the floor with the spine marking the division of the two halves of the body. Determine if, by doing that, you can bring your spine into a clearer focus. Now stop.

Lie there with your feet standing, separated at least a little bit. Once again try to sense your spine and to breathe up and along it as if you could breathe into it. Follow your spine all the way up as if you could breathe up and down your spine.

Flex your ankles and breathe out through your teeth with a hissing sound. As you do that, extend your legs, leaving your back flat on the floor and finally releasing your ankles. Once again, try to sense the spine in the middle.

Now bring your hands in as close to your body as they will comfortably lie with the palms down and the elbows straight. Take your arms above your head on the floor. Observe where and how your arms lie. Notice how close to your ears your arms can comfortably lie, and whether you have to bend your elbows or if you can keep your elbows straight. Do you have to bend your wrists, or can you keep them straight and still make contact with the floor? Do it the best you can without bending your elbows, whether your arms touch the floor or not and regardless of how close they come to your ears.

Now put your arms out at your sides at shoulder height with

your palms down. Slide your palms along the floor, pushing them away from you and then bringing them back, moving from the shoulders without bending your elbows. Do it smoothly and easily. It does not matter how extensive a movement it is. You will see that it will increase greatly as the work progresses.

Now put your extended arms down at your sides and slide the palms along the floor, sliding them down towards your toes and then bringing them back up. That is a much more familiar movement so you do it more extensively, but the other one can be made much more extensively also. Do it smoothly and easily.

When your arms were at shoulder height, they were at right angles to the arms, as they are now. There are 90-degree angles that separate the arm as it now is from the arm at shoulder height. Move the arm out to midpoint at about a 45-degree angle from your body. Try to sense accurately that that is where it is, that it is not too close to the shoulder-height position and not too close to the legs either. Then slide your hand away and bring it back, moving from your shoulders.

Having done that, extend your arms at shoulder height. Continue to slide the palms across the floor away from you and then back again. Do it in a smooth way and breathe freely. Stop and rest with your arms at shoulder height.

Now, once again, consider that when the hands are above the head, the arms at shoulder height are in the same relation to those arms, in terms of the angles and degrees, as they are to the arms when the arms are down at your sides. If your arms were directly overhead, the arms as they are now would be at a 90-degree or right angle to the arms above the head. Move your arms up by 45 degrees. Try to sense clearly the midpoint between shoulder height and arms above the head. Now look a moment and see if your arms are really where you felt that they were, that they really are at midpoint between shoulder height and the arms fully above the head. You may find that you need to place your hands with the palms up to make it easier. Determine if it is easier with the palms up.

Once again slide your hands along the floor and bring them back, pushing and pulling from your shoulders. Look at them and see if they are really up high enough. See if each arm is the same. If they are not at the proper height, is it because you can do no better or because you are sensing wrong? Bring them as close to the proper angle as you can. Then let them rest there.

Do a few more movements, but on the outside edge of your hands. Do not do it on the tops of the hands, but try it on the edges where the little finger is. Slide your arms and hands back and forth along the floor. The movement is all in the shoulders. Do both of them simultaneously as before. It is exactly the same movement as when your arms are down at your sides.

Now put your arms out at shoulder height and rest. Note if it is more restful to have your palms down or palms up. Just examine the alternatives and see which one feels better to you.

Then raise your two arms towards the ceiling. Lower them over your head as close to your ears as you can. Notice where they go. Repeat this several times. Bring your arms together so that as you lower them they slide off your cheekbones and come to rest alongside your ears.

Then, wherever your arms are, slide your hands up and down along the floor from the shoulders. It is the same movement that you have been making all along. The hands go up and down along the floor. In almost every case, it will be easier if the backs of the hands are on the floor. It is impossible to put the palms down. You can put part of them down, but to do it all is very hard. Just keep pushing and pulling with your shoulders as long as it is not painful. If it is painful, stop doing it. Now put your arms down at your sides again.

You have seen, most likely in the religion and mythology of India, figures of Deities having many arms. The following exercise is called Making the Body with Twelve Arms. If you succeed, you will create a body image with twelve arms that can be held simultaneously in awareness. Maybe you will only do four or six or eight or ten the first time, but you will create such a body. When you have done it, then you will find that the shoulders have been further released and that some other quite interesting things have happened in terms of improving the functioning of your shoulders and their mobility as well.

Now your arms should be at your sides with your palms down. Sense them clearly. Then move them up and down along the floor, keeping the elbows straight. Do it smoothly.

Now stop and sense your arms and hands clearly. Observe how well you can bring them into your awareness.

Bring your arms up to 45 degrees, midway between shoulder height and down at your sides. Then push and pull from your shoulders as before, your hands just sliding along the floor. Try to sense clearly, and make certain that your arms are neither too high nor too low. Look at your two arms and see if they are actually symmetrical or if one hand is closer to the body than the other hand. When you see that they are symmetrical, note whether you also feel it. Then continue to slide the hands along the floor away from you and then towards you, moving from the shoulders.

Now rest in that 45-degree-angle position and sense clearly how your arms lie. Make them as clear as possible in your body image.

Then *image* at the same time two arms lying at your sides. Imagine or image moving the hands up and down lying at your sides. Now focus on the (objective) arms as they are, lying at a 45-degree angle.

Then, retaining that image and sensory impression, put the hands back down at the sides. Now sense the arms lying at your sides, and also image them lying out where they just were. Imagine the hands and the arms at a 45-degree angle moving back and forth along the floor. The feeling is in the shoulders, the arms, the hands. Slide those imaginal arms back and forth along the floor. Then let them rest and sense them simultaneously with the arms that are at your sides. Now make a few movements up and down with the hands of your physical body, sliding them up and down along the floor. "Up and down" means in terms of your feet and your head unless otherwise defined. It is in terms of your own physical being and not the room around you. Now sense that clearly.

Stop and sense the arms as they are. Bring them out to a 45-degree angle. Sense that. Slide them back and forth along the floor a few times. Now stop and sense the physical arms where they are, and also try to sense or image clearly arms that are down at your sides.

Then put your physical arms out at shoulder height. Try to sense whether they are actually at shoulder height. Do a visual check to see if it is so, but always sense it first. Then having adjusted them according to your visual sensing, note if it feels right or if it still feels that it would be a better sensing if the arms were as they were before you corrected them. Now sense the arms as they are and sense or imagine arms at a 45-degree angle to your body, and also sense them as lying down alongside your legs.

Image your arms down at your sides with your hands moving along the floor, up and down. What would that feel like? Then imagine or image doing it at the 45-degree angle, moving the palms up and down along the floor. Now make that actual movement at shoulder height, sliding your hands away from you and back towards you. Make it as extensive a movement as possible. Move both arms simultaneously, away and then back. Do it quickly. Now stop.

Try to sense the three positions again—the arms as they are, the arms at your sides, and the arms at the point in between. Then raise them another 45 degrees. Let them be with either the palms or the backs on the floor, whichever feels better. Try to sense your arms clearly as they lie now, and also sense the image of your body with the arms lying out at shoulder height. Try to feel how the arms go side to side at shoulder height. Then sense the arms 45 degrees lower, both how they lie and how they feel moving with the palms of the hands up and down along the floor. Then sense how the arms feel down at the sides. Feel that they are lying down at your sides and the hands are moving up and down along the floor.

Now slide your hands along the floor physically, extending and retracting them. If you are doing it on the backs of your hands, try doing it on the palms. Then do it whichever way feels better to you. Your physical arms are at a 45-degree angle above the shoulder-height position. Leave them there and just move them out and back along the floor. Note visually again the position of your arms. Try to make that movement light and quick. Now stop.

Sense your arms as they are. Sense image arms out at shoulder height. Sense others down just 45 degrees away from your legs. Then sense others alongside your body. Now place the physical arms in that position, palms down alongside your body.

Rest a moment. Determine if you can just sense them there while having a clear image of how your arms feel out at shoulder height.

At shoulder height, sense an image of moving them, sliding the hands out away from you and back towards you.

Then have an image of doing it at a point midway between the hands at the sides and shoulder height. Image sliding them along the floor.

Then image arms above your head at a 45-degree angle above the shoulder-height position, probably lying on the backs of the hands now. Sense that, and move them out and back. Let them lie up there and at shoulder height and out at your sides 45 degrees and down at your sides.

Then raise your physical arms and place them above your head on the floor. Bring the hands up to point to the ceiling and let one wrist cross the other one. Then bring them down overhead. See if you can keep it that way and if the arms make an easy contact with the ears or come much closer than they did.

Then try crossing the wrists the other way, and bring them up to the ceiling. Then bring them down.

Now with your hands above your head, take hold of your elbows so that your arms are in contact with the ears, or as close to them as you can easily come. Keeping the arms in as close to your ears as you can hold them without straining, bring them up a number of times so that the elbows are parallel to the floor, and then let them down above your head again. Keep bringing your arms in towards your ears, however close they can easily come.

Then let go of the elbows and cross the arms so that the arms come in even closer to the ears. Do that, letting the arms slide down off your face. Let them come as close to the floor as they will. Take them away and do it again. Keep raising and lowering them. Put first one wrist on top and then the other. Do a few one way and a few the other way.

Then do it without crossing your wrists. Just raise both hands to the ceiling. Let your wrists be loose and let your arms come down alongside your ears to the extent that they will. When your arms touch the floor overhead, or as close to it as they will come, stop there.

Push your arms up and down so that your hands slide along the floor, moving up and down from the shoulders. Then stop a minute.

Sense your arms as they lie. Get a clear impression of them. Then leave the image of the arms on the floor above you as you physically move them down to your sides. Rest, but sense your arms overhead and your arms at your sides.

Now slide your hands vigorously up and down so that they move down as far as they will go. Make the movement as extensive as you can. Let your legs be extended. Note how far down you can reach and how far up the shoulders will go. Without straining, determine how far down and how far up your arms go.

Now extend them at a 45-degree angle and slide the hands along the floor. Examine the mobility in the shoulders. Slide the hands away and back. Make the movement as extensive as possible.

If for some reason it is painful, stop and image doing it. Otherwise, continue to do it and know how extensively and quickly and lightly you can make that movement. Now stop.

Extend your physical arms out at shoulder height. Once again, slide your hands along the floor. Make it as extensive and as quick and as light as you can. Ascertain if now that movement has a kind of clarity in the shoulders that it did not have before so that it is easier to make a more extensive movement. Bring the hands out and back. Slide them along the floor at shoulder height. Be sure that it is at shoulder height. Then rest for a minute. Now do a few more actual movements at shoulder height, as extensively as you can without straining. Observe how far out you can reach and how far back you can come. Then stop.

Now image doing it with the arms down 45 degrees. Image or imagine making as extensive an arm-sliding movement as you can. Then image doing it with your hands at your sides and the shoulders moving down and up as the arms and hands slide along the floor.

Image doing the movements simultaneously with your arms at your sides, out 45 degrees and at shoulder height. Try to begin with one image and add on another and then a third. If you cannot do three, then you can do two. If you cannot do two, do one. Do it well, and then add the second and the third. Image movements that get quicker and lighter and easier and more extensive. Image movements that are really fast and moving farther.

Now physically place your arms in as perfect a 45-degree angle between shoulder height and the arms-above-the-head position as you can get them. Visually check it to see if they are high enough and if they are the same on both sides.

Now, with your arms up as close to a perfect 45-degree angle as you can get them, form an image of them lying out at your sides at shoulder height. Then form an image of other arms lying down 45 degrees, and another of arms lying alongside your legs. Try to hold that image, and make a second image of the arms out at 45 degrees and a third image of the arms up at shoulder height, holding all three images and sensing your arms as they now are.

Slide your right arm on up along the floor to beside your ear and leave it there, as close as you can get while it is still on the floor. Then slide your left arm up towards the other ear. Then raise both arms overhead towards the ceiling, and let them come back down over your face. Notice if they will lie alongside your ears. Also let the backs of your hands lie on the floor if they will, or as much as they will. Then slide them up and down along the floor, moving from your shoulders.

Now stop and sense that. Lie with your arms in the closest possible proximity to your ears and with as much contact on the floor as possible. Sense how you lie, and remember what you have observed.

Take hold of your elbows with your hands. Then just fold your arms across your chest, taking hold of your upper arms with your hands. Now try to get an image of the arms above the head as they were a moment ago, and a second image of the arms down 45 degrees from that so that they are lying on the floor at a midpoint between the arms above the head and the shoulder-height positions. Then put the arms in your imaging out at shoulder height. Then image them down 45 degrees further with the hands out a bit from the legs. Then image your hands at your sides, palms down. Also sense them as they presently physically are.

Now determine how many of those arms you can bring into your awareness at once. Try to sense or image the arms down at your sides. Then try to image them another 45 degrees up while keeping the image of the arms at the sides. Then add on to that an image of the arms at shoulder height. Maintain all of those images in your awareness. Image your arms up another 45 degrees, and then image lastly your arms above your head. Sense your arms on your chest. To the extent that you can bring all those images into your consciousness and hold them, you have made The Body With Twelve Arms. Now put your physical arms down at your sides again.

Keep your elbows straight. Push down and pull up with your shoulders quickly. Take the shoulders down as far as you can go without straining, and then let them come just a little bit up. Continue making the movements, gradually bringing the hands and arms out from your body a little more with each movement or each few movements. You start at your sides and gradually move away until you eventually work up to shoulder height and above and on up to over your head. At whatever point your hands must turn over onto their backs, let them do it.

When you have finally reached the position above your head, then come back down again, and once again in small gradations so that you move the shoulders from as many different points as possible. Move them only an inch or two at a time from their previous position. Take them up towards overhead and then back down towards being at your sides. Each movement will, of course, make a different demand on the shoulders and will give the shoulders experiences of movement and shadings of movement that they do not ordinarily get.

You are at a point where some of the most important Work now can be done. If you must stop and image, do so, but keep moving from your shoulders, either with the physical body or the imaged body.

Now once more, fold your physical arms on your chest. Try to image the twelve arms. Begin with the two down at your sides, and then image the two out at 45 degrees, and the two at shoulder height, and the two up another 45 degrees, and the two above your head, and sense the two now resting on your chest. Take your time. Try to use the movements from the shoulders to vivify each image in succession before you add the next one. Note how many of them you can add.

Continue to practice, using any means that you can devise.Try to reach the twelve. Get the most vivid impressions that you can of how your arms feel lying in each position, both how they feel lying still and how they feel when you move them. When you try to bring as many as possible into your awareness, it is usually easier to do it with the arms unmoving. When you can move ten of them while the other two lie across the chest, then you have succeeded with the mental part of the exercise and the greatest physical benefits will be forthcoming.

Now, once more put your physical arms down at your sides. Slide your physical arms up and down so that they go down just as far as they go. Notice how extensive the movements can be now. If you can, take them further than you could before, without arching your back as you do it. Again, observe how extensive the movements can be, and how quick and light. You should be able to sense that you reach further down than you ordinarily do.

Put your arms out at your sides at shoulder height and slide the palms along the floor as extensively as you can. Notice if there is a mobility and a clarity in the idea of moving your arms back and forth at shoulder height which was quite absent at the beginning of this exercise. Observe how quickly and easily you can do it.

Once more take your arms up toward the ceiling. Let your hands touch lightly, one on top of the other. Let them go down, sliding off the cheekbones and then coming to rest alongside your ears.

Then place the arms alongside the head, palms up, with the arms as close to your ears as possible. Not how that is as compared to what you did in the beginning. Raise them once more and let them come down alongside your ears. Let them come off the face and onto the floor. Now, bring your arms down alongside your body and rest.

Observe how your shoulders are in relation to the floor and how your hands and your arms are lying. Then slowly roll to one side and get up.

Walk around, letting your arms move freely. Take note of what your shoulders feel. Try various movements with the arms—raising them and letting go, making circles, twisting side to side. Note carefully what your shoulders feel like—if they feel light and the movement is effortless, or much less effortful than before. Raise each arm, and if that is much easier as far as your shoulder is concerned, then you have accomplished a good deal. Now just lie down again.

If you want to once more observe how you can put your hands above your head on the floor and compare that to what you did before, do it. Then just lie still again.

One final time, try to make the twelve arms, but make them a little differently. This time, you will sense the arms down at your sides and image them up 45 degrees, image them at shoulder height, image them up another 45 degrees, image them above your head, and image them folded over your chest. Once again, use images of the movements as well as just remembering how it felt for them to lie passively in those different positions.

Now let the images go except for the body image that should correspond as closely as possible to your physical body lying on the floor. Try to sense your body just as clearly as you can. Go over it. Note what parts are clearest in your body image. Sense how your shoulders lie, your arms, your hands and the small of your back. If you need to, flatten it. Let your feet stand and raise your pelvis a few times and put the lower back down flat on the floor. Observe whether, without doing that, it is not lying flatter than it usually does with the shoulders also lower.

Breathe a few times up through your middle and out through the top of your head and down along the center line, the hypothetical line that begins between your legs and runs straight up through the middle and on out through the top of your head.

Then, for a minute, hold the top of your head in your hands and breathe up toward your hands. At the same time explore the top of your head with your hands.

Then let the consciousness move up for a moment into the brain space under the hands. Breathe up into that space. For a while, breathe through your nose into the space. Then it is as if you can breathe through your eyes into it, and as if you could breathe through your ears into it. Then just breathe up and up into the top of your head so that your whole body elongates somewhat. The neck lengthens and your spine lengthens. Then, without stiffening your neck, come to a sitting position.

With your eyes closed, continue to breathe up into the top of your head. Do it with the feeling that the head elongates and the whole body is drawn upward by the breathing. Focus on your brain space and feel that your neck actually lengthens. Everything tends to move up. Then again, slowly roll to one side and get up without using your head and neck to initiate the movement. Do it in whatever way is best for you.

Move around for a while, breathing up through the top of your head. Feel as if the head and the neck and everything moves up— the whole body lengthens.

Then, for a little while, sense the shoulders. Raise them and notice how light the feeling is in the shoulders, and how little effort it takes to raise your arms.

EXPERIENCING
THE DOUBLE—
AN INTRODUCTION

Walk around for a while. As you walk, try to bring your whole body image into awareness. Keep in mind, just as clearly as you can, all of the sensations involved in the walking. Be aware of what you are doing with your head, your eyes. Do this with the fullest amount of consciousness that you are able to bring to bear on your activity, with everything that you have learned about your use of yourself, and with the highest level of consciousness that you are capable of as you move. Now, stop moving with your physical body.

Project an image body that walks around the room. Try to feel all of the sensations of that body. Observe it. Try to let it walk as you have been walking. Use your memory to project the image of yourself outside of yourself. Observe the way that the image body walks, what its behavior is. What quality of consciousness would you attribute to it?

Try to get the clearest possible image of yourself moving around the room. Observe it in an objective and detached way. What is your opinion of the use, the functioning and quality of consciousness of that being you now observe? See if, observing and projecting that image, you can improve it. Analyze it. Take careful note of its strong and weak points, its successes and failures. Try to let it really represent the best of what you have learned and know.

Next, move with your objective body. Move with the highest

quality of consciousness. Move with awareness of the best use that you have been able to project into the body image. Observe if your movement is really identical with the movement of the image. Try to recall it and make it the same. Then come back and lie down.

Scan your body. Again, see how fully you can bring it into your mind. Bring the body into the mind and the mind into the body so that the mind and the body are experienced as one. Now, endeavoring to keep the mind and the body unified—the physical body on the floor mindful—again project out of yourself and let an image of your body rise and walk around. Make that body also as mindful as possible so that you sense its movements, its contact with the floor, what it is hearing, what it is seeing, what it is thinking and feeling. But preserve your awareness of the body-mind lying on the floor.

Allow yourself to go into trance. Your consciousness should alter as profoundly as it needs to in order to achieve the awareness of the two bodies. Maintain one consciousness in the body that lies on the floor and another consciousness simultaneously in the body that moves around the room so that you can sense the body lying on the floor and the movements and the contact, hearing, seeing, feeling of the body that moves around. That body that moves around the room should not be a body that differs in appearance or sensations or mode of functioning from the physical body. *It should be its Double*. The two bodies should be *exactly alike*.

Let that body come and stand and look at the body that is lying on the floor. At the same time, the body that is lying on the floor is looking out through eyes that are closed or, if possible, eyes that are open at the body that is standing above it so that the two bodies and the two consciousnesses regard each other simultaneously. The body on the floor observes the body that is standing, and the body that is standing observes the body that is lying. Each mind is conscious of the other.

Now, this body—this Double—to the extent that you can put your consciousness into it, your sensations into it, move around with it—can, by its actions, directly affect the physical body. The physical body is a reflection of the Double that you experience, and the Double that you experience is a reflection of the physical body. It is also true, to the extent that the two bodies are reflections of each other, that what you do with the physical body will affect the reflected image, or the Double.

It is easy to understand why you would want to use the image body to bring about changes in the physical body. It is important to learn why you would want to do the opposite—use the physical body to bring about changes in the image. There are good reasons to do it. Eventually, you will have the experience of how and why it should be done. But for now, let the image body lie down alongside the physical body. What that image body does has consequences that are quite different from imagining movements of the actual physical body.

Now let the two bodies lie side by side. Move the right side of the imaged body—the Double. Move it in many, many different ways. Rotate the legs in and out. Move the legs up and down. Move the toes, the fingers, the ankles, the wrists, the knees, the elbows, the hip joints and the shoulders. Perform many, many movements with the right side only of the Double—the image body. Take two to three minutes of clock time, during which the image body—the Double—can carry out a very, very large number of different movements and many repetitions of each movement. Do as many different movements with the right side as you are able to conceive. You will have a long time to do those many, many, many movements. You have that time *now*.

Be increasingly aware *just* of the movements of the image body. The physical body, at most, is only an observer. It is the image body that senses and feels and has a life of its own. Now, to the extent that you can do this well, you can make much more far-reaching changes in the physical body by working on the Double than you can by imaging the actions of the physical body.

Now, when we imagine the actions of the physical body, we will change it to some extent. To imagine actions done with another body or bodies may change those other bodies to some extent. Once you have been able to create an image body, and to use it to transform the physical body, then you have taken the first step towards going beyond fantasy—what Paracelsus called "that cornerstone of fools"—into the true realm of imaginal action that is the beginning of psychic, paranormal or magical functioning—and The Way of the Five Bodies and of the magician-priest or -priestess. When you can do it, you will see that the effects are as scientifically verifiable as anything having to do with the physical body.

Just as you can experience a Double of your own body, so you can experience the Double of another body or of other bodies. You can learn to extract from another body a Double of that body and interact with it. In fact, this is what, at the lowest level of psychic development, a psychic does, whether for healing, for defense against psychic attack, or in an unscrupulous way to attack by psychic means. To simply imagine and try to telepathically transmit in that way your wishes to the physical body of another person is just as easy to do as to fantasize about your own body. On the other hand, to extract a Double of that other body and to act on it is a much more potent way of functioning. When you can do it and fully sense the interaction between the two Doubles, then you will find that your ability to do psychic healing and your ability to do such things as defend yourself against psychic attack will be greatly enhanced.

To begin, place your consciousness as fully as possible in your Double. Then, thinking of any other person of your choosing, try to experience an image of that person that is extracted from the physical body—that is, a Double of that person, just as your own image body is the Double of your physical body. It takes a good deal of work in the beginning to do that.

Determine if you can do it. Take any other person that you like, someone you want to have a healing effect on or that you want to affect in some constructive way. First, recall that person's actual physical body. Next, experience a Double of that body. Then, with your Double, interact with that Double so that you can sense not only the internal feelings of your own image—your mirror image or Double—but you can touch and be aware of the sensations and feelings in that other body. As ordinary, objective bodies interact, so let those Doubles interact. Spend quite a bit of time doing it. It is a complex and novel undertaking.

Choose a person that you *want* to interact with. Instead of just fantasizing about your body interacting with the physical body of that person, as is ordinarily done, experience two Doubles and let the two Doubles interact with the intention that the effect upon the Double will be reflected in its physical body. Know that this is true both for yourself and for the other.

It can be done at higher levels of consciousness and with subtler bodies. In mystery traditions, this is how magicians interact on magical planes; at lower levels, astral bodies, etheric bodies project and interact. At the highest levels, higher magical or spiritual bodies meet and interact not only with one another but with beings that never, or almost never, come down into the lower dimensions. The consciousness must *ascend* to meet them, but the beginning is to experience the Doubles and let the Doubles interact.

Again, it is possible to do it better if you go into trance and go deep, deeply into trance so that the Double becomes more and more real—both your own Double and that of the person with whom you have the interaction. Also, in the trance you have a great deal of subjective time within a much smaller unit of clock time than would be possible otherwise. In this undertaking, you will have five minutes of clock-measured time during which you can very carefully select and, as completely as possible, extract from the physical body—or enable it to rise out of the physical body of the other person—a Double with which you can interact with sensory awareness and interchange of feelings and thoughts, performing some *constructive action* upon that Double which will be reflected in its physical or lower physical reality. You have that time *now*.

Now, if you have succeeded to even some extent, you can understand how prolonged practice of such psychospiritual work lays the foundation for being able to disengage the Double and get other more subtle bodies from the gross physical body; how it facilitates the ability to move into other dimensions of reality that could only be experienced largely as fantasy were it not for the ability of the Double and of the other subtle bodies to actually sense and experience. This Work also can be used to help awaken and integrate subtle bodies.

Now, finally, just finding yourself alone and in a space, stand and observe that the space is circular and that there can come and stand beside you a great lion—a numinous, archetypal figure of a lion. Look around the circle at its outer edges, and see if you can become aware of those dark shapes and forms that represent some of the forces that are impinging on you from without—from negative emotions, or thoughts of other persons—or they may be your own projections; see whether those forms are frightening or how frightening they might be. Try to see them clearly.

Walk with the confidence that the lion will not only protect you but will diminish those forces around you, whether they emanate from within or from without. In any case, whatever their source, their reality is inside of your own unconscious mind, and that is where they work on your brain and your consciousness.

Walk with the lion around the circle into and all around the outer edge where you have passed, and leave a circle of light. You are able to confront the forms of darkness. Do it, until they vanish in the light. You complete the circle with the lion at your side.

Continue until you have done that. Then return to the center of the circle, observing the circle of light all round, knowing that you have formed a powerful protective shield around yourself and that you can repeat this operation. The more powerful the awareness of the Double and its sensations, the more powerful that Double will be in your unconscious mind and in your body, and the greater its effect will be in protecting you against all manner of evil or disruptive forces. You can learn to use this mirror image body's reflection or Double in many, many, many ways. With practice, you will be able to work also with higher manifestations, subtler bodies, and do much more powerful Work—the Work of a real School.

In esoteric Teachings, penalties for using a body such as the Double to interact upon other bodies in illicit or non-defensive, destructive ways are called Karmic penalties. It means that you will be damaged in future incarnations as well as in this one, and the higher and subtler the body that commits the offense, the more incarnations the penalties extend through. Whether you want to put it that way or some other way, it is a cosmic law or truth that is being stated because the possibilities of affecting other people once you are able to do a thing like this are very, very great.

You will go into the unconscious, and it is also possible for two developed beings, as I mentioned, to meet on this level and higher levels and to engage in experiences and share them that are quite impossible in the gross material realm where almost all human experience that is ever conscious is had. You may dream about this. You will certainly think about it further, and you should try to grasp more of the implications. You now have the means, if you are able to use them, to detach the Double from the gross physical body and make it conscious.

Now, you will have two minutes of clock time to let the Double merge again with the physical body so that you have a sense only of being one mindful body, one psychophysical unity, but with an awareness of some of the potencies of that entity which, unless you have experienced them before, you had, at best, an abstract notion of. You have two minutes now to allow that integration to occur and then to wake up and feel your mind and body at one. You have that time *now*.

When the integration and reunification are complete, simply stretch and come to a sitting or standing position. Then move around, feeling awake and well.

Whether you were able to experience the Double the first time or not, remember at least the possibility of how you might go about it.

ORCHESTRATING MULTISENSORY AWARENESSES

This exercise will clearly recognize, differentiate, and then orchestrate many sensory awarenesses—with a result that can be quite astonishing. You will learn how using one sense affects the use of another sense, and also how one activity affects another activity. You will learn whether a sensory experience is diluted by engaging in another activity or by primarily using another sense. But at the same time, you will use sensory impressions as a "food"—to strengthen Being and Presence.

You will work mainly with five senses: the kinesthetic sense—the sense of movement—and four traditional senses: the tactile or touching sense; the sense of hearing; the sense of vision; and, possibly to a lesser extent, the sense of smell. You will observe that when you focus on your kinesthetic sense it will be much easier to do so with your eyes closed. When you open your eyes and continue the movement and begin to try to focus your vision on something, you will see that one of these senses is purchased at the expense of the other sense. If you focus on the movement more, then you will not sense the seeing as clearly. In the same way, if you try to focus on the tactile sense, the contact of your body with the environment, and then simultaneously focus on either movement or vision or hearing, you will find that whichever of these you give your main attention to will dilute the other one(s).

201

Is this because you *cannot sense* simultaneously and equally with your various senses, or is the dilution occurring because you are trying *to do more* than one thing at once? You can make a case for the dilution by a division of attention because you can try to sense your movements. For instance, while thinking about some very complicated problem, you will find that you cannot give your full attention to the thinking and the sensing at the same time. One detracts from the other. It is a division of attention. This is the common mode of functioning of human beings as we are today. However, this division is not something that is necessary.

There are techniques in different cultures that allow people to do or to sense a number of things simultaneously with full attention apparently given to each, without one taking anything away from the other. We also find that ability in the case of children, insofar as we can determine it. People living closer to a natural state can give their sensory awareness to several senses at once without one appearing to detract from the other.

What we will do first is try to make you fully aware of how divisions of attention and simultaneous use of the senses dilute some aspect of your sensory or intellectual experience. Then, after that, we will try to orchestrate the sensory awarenesses so that you can move and use several senses at the same time and not feel that you are using one at the expense of the other. In other words, we will try to break down a very deeply ingrained pattern of behavior and show that, although it is virtually universal, it is a habit and not a necessity. In a healthy human being who is aware of what he/she is doing, and who is able to function at a higher level of consciousness, all the senses can be used simultaneously.

Begin by lying on your back and bending your legs so that your feet are standing. Place your feet a short distance apart. Then take your legs gently from side to side, your feet remaining on the floor. Sense primarily movement. As you continue to do this basic movement throughout a good part of the exercise, try to make it a more and more pleasurable one. You will find as your spine gets more and more flexible and the muscles longer and looser that pleasure sensations will increasingly come.

Perform this movement for a while with your eyes closed. In fact, unless asked to do something with your eyes open, keep them closed so that you do not have an inadvertent rivalry of the senses. The competitions between them are kept as minimal as possible except for those that the exercise is designed to encourage.

Now, as you take your legs from side to side, take your head also from side to side. Notice if it seems to you that you are equally aware kinesthetically of the movement of your lower body and the movement of your head. Are you more aware of the lower body movement or the head movement?

Now, deliberately give a larger part of your awareness to the lower body movement, the movement of your legs side to side and the movement that you experience in your lower spine as you lie on your back and take your legs side to side. You continue to move your head, but you give your awareness mostly to the lower body movements.

Then, instead of giving your awareness to your lower body, you give it to your head. Make that somewhat easier by opposing the head movements to the leg movements. Now continue to give your main awareness to the head and neck movements, but allow the head and the legs to go in the same direction. Also include in that upper body awareness the movement in your shoulders and in your upper back.

Then, determine if it is presently possible for you to equalize your sensing so that what you sense when you turn your head from side to side is equally as clear in your mind as what you sense when you take your legs from side to side. Your upper body movement ideally should be neither more nor less clear than your lower body movement. And you should be able to say that the kinesthetic sense is equally apprehended throughout your body. Even though your mind is not favoring one part at the expense of the other, if you sense subtly enough, if you discriminate enough in your sensing, you will find that it is an extremely difficult thing to sense equally the lower and the upper body movements. Here you are working with a division within one sense and with a coordinated movement, the legs and the head going from one side to the other simultaneously. This is an optimal condition, really, for being able to sense equally and kinesthetically the movements that the body is making. Lie down on your back and rest with your arms at your sides. Scan your body image.

Now, open your eyes and give your visual attention to something just as fully as you can. Look at something visually arresting. You might try to pick out images in the patterns on the ceiling. Try to see as clearly as you can color, form, texture, shadings of light and dark. Find something you can give full visual attention to.

Then, bend your legs and take them side to side, maintaining the visual focus. From that sensory standpoint, your interest is in what you see and not in the kinesthetic or tactile sensations in your lower body. Try to make certain that you do not inhibit your breathing, but do not pay any particular attention to it. Only the visual sense is what you are concerned with.

Now, maintain your visual focus but also give a large measure of attention to the kinesthetic movement of your legs from side to side. Sense your leg movements, and try to do so without sacrificing the eye sensing. Observe whether it seems to you that you are able to sense kinesthetically as completely as possible while also looking with your eyes. Make the kinesthetic sensing as keen as you can, but any time you experience any dilution of the visual sensing, try to get that back.

Now, close your eyes and continue to move from side to side. Pay attention to the sensations of movement. Note if you are able to perceive very clearly that the sensation is now stronger than when your eyes were open. Vision was taking something away from the sense of movement. As you continue to take your legs side to side, observe how keenly you can sense that movement.

Open your eyes and observe whether you can preserve the same degree of sensing with your eyes open or if you find it diluted.

Now, just let your legs stand. Focus on something with your eyes. Use your visual sense just as clearly and as fully as you are able to do. Bring the object of your perception into focus. Continue to try to see more and more clearly and completely.

Then, as you continue to use your visual capacity as completely as you are able, take your legs from side to side. Observe for how long you are able to maintain that same visual clarity while you move. Try to give your full awareness to the scene. Now, try to equalize the vision and the movement so that you give equal attention to each one. Try to arrive at a balance where you feel that your visual and kinesthetic senses are being used equally.

Then, gradually let your eyes go out of focus and observe what happens with the kinesthetic sensing. Then, close your eyes about halfway so that there is still light but you are not able to see any object. All you see is a kind of undifferentiated light. Note what effect that has on the sensation of movement.

Next, close your eyes and continue to move your lower body.

Notice if that intensifies the kinesthetic sensation still further. A few times let your head and your legs go together. Remark if you can give a more equal amount of sensing to both movements now. Is there the same need or a lesser need to take something away from one part of your body because the other part is moving? Or as far as the kinesthetic sensing goes, is the body a bit more unified and better integrated? Then, just lie down and rest.

Let your hands be palms down at your sides and your arms extended. Examine the clarity of your body image, or lack of clarity. Note how it is now and compare it with how it was at the beginning. Remember how it is now so that you can compare it with how it will be a bit later on.

Now, just roll your head gently from side to side. Pay attention to the sensations involved in the rolling. Then divert your attention from the kinesthetic to your tactile sense. In other words, pay attention to what your body is touching and to the contact with it. Deemphasize the movement and pay attention to the sense of touch. Note your interaction with the surface beneath you, both insofar as your head is concerned and also the rest of your body lying on the floor, but pay most attention to what the head touches. As you emphasize the tactile sense, observe how that affects the kinesthetic one, or the sensations of movement.

Divert your attention back to movement. Do not be concerned with the sensation of touch. Notice what you feel kinesthetically. Notice whether now that sensation increases while the tactile sense is accordingly diminished or, if you will, impoverished, diluted. Give all your attention, or as much of it as you can, to the feelings of movement.

Then, return your attention to what you touch, the interaction between the external world and your own body where it impinges on you and you on it. That is what your consciousness is mainly concerned with. Continue to turn your head. Let your consciousness be aware of the floor and your head's contact with the floor and of your body lying on the floor. Notice whether there is any way in which you can balance the internal and external so that you can sense the interaction between yourself and the objective world through the tactile sense. Sense your movements without one taking anything away from the other.

Rest your head and leave your elbows straight. Slide your hands up and down along the floor at your sides. Emphasize the feelings of movement in your body. Then shift from a kinesthetic to a tactile awareness so that your awareness is of the contact with the surface beneath you, primarily of your hands and arms, but also the rest of your body. You need only be sufficiently aware to know that you are moving; your primary interest is in touch. Then compare what you sense now with what you sensed when you were giving your consciousness to the kinesthetic sense.

Now, give your consciousness back to the kinesthetic sense again. Your awareness is of movement. You have little concern with the touching or the being touched. Observe whether being concerned with movement not only brings the kinesthetic sensation into sharper focus, but seems to cause you to spontaneously increase the movement.

Go back to tactile awareness once again. Now, divide that awareness so that for a time you orient yourself towards what you are touching, towards learning about the world outside, primarily, and then for a while you orient yourself to what the hand is feeling, the greater attention being paid to the self. Notice the difference—a division that is within the tactile sense and the shifts of orientation. Then just pay attention to the sense of touch, without being concerned about dividing it between awareness of self and not-self. Finally, go back to sensing movement once again. Then, stop and rest.

Scan your body image for a little while and then try recapitulating in your mind some of what you have been doing. Those of you who can perceive visual images with the eyes closed might try alternating between those and kinesthetic images. Imagine or image moving your legs from side to side. If you do not have visual images that you see as you see the images on a movie screen, for example, nevertheless imagine looking at whatever you were focused on in the room. Image taking your legs side to side. Shift your attention from your visual imaginary focus to your kinesthetic imagery.

Then, open your eyes and focus on some actual object that you can see clearly. Bring that object into the clearest possible focus. Then, as you endeavor to keep your focus on that object, silently recite to yourself some piece of poetry or prose that you know well, like the Gettysburg Address. If you cannot manage that, at least some nursery rhyme or children's piece of poetry, scripture or whatever it may be. Recite that while endeavoring to maintain the visual focus. Carefully note any blurring of parts of it, any loss of detail. Also, try singing to yourself. Notice whether you can maintain your clear visual focus and for how long and in what way it changes. Now, stop once again and establish a visual focus, something very clear. Identify the parts of that visual sensing so that when anything changes you know it and can recognize it clearly.

You now will be provided with first one kind of auditory stimulus, talking. Then you will be provided with another kind. Listen as carefully as you can, whether it seems to make sense or not, while doing all that you can, apart from holding your breath or tightening your muscles, to maintain your seeing. See as clearly as possible.

Now listen with great intensity as we deliberate over whether the exercise is designed to speak about the Aristotelian sublunary theory of the vegetative soul, or the Leibnitzian notion of monads, or the concept of the will in Schopenhauer and Nietzsche, whether the exercise is designed to speak about Platonic ideas, aesthetics or possibly Bergson's *Elan Vital,* or perhaps Hartshorne's theory of sensory affective continuity. Or we might want to talk about the second law of thermodynamics. We might want to talk about certain ideas of Einstein or of Heidegger. And we might talk about Being and Nothingness and about the transiency of reality, about what reality is, and about those experiments where animals who have learned a maze can be killed with their brains fed to other animals who never learned the maze. By eating the brain of the animal who learned it, the fed animal learns to go through the maze without any other kind of training.

We might want to talk about the experiments of a man called Rupert Sheldrake, who is in a sense repeating the experiments done long ago by Rudolph Steiner. Sheldrake has shown that if one group of rats learns to run a particular maze anywhere in the world, then some other rats elsewhere can run that particular maze better than they could before. The time of the learning is reduced for the other rats. The same thing is claimed to be true for other kinds of animals as well. Once a particular learning enters into the consciousness of a species, it appears to be transferred to the consciousness of other members of the same species. This might account for the recurrence of the same myths, mythologies and religions of different peoples in different times and places throughout the world that up to now has baffled historians and psychologists.

Try to maintain your visual focus as this spoken discussion goes on and on, probably making no sense to you, but offering competition with that visual sense, and perceive that your reality has indeed been affected—that your ability to maintain your visual focus is affected by both your conscious and unconscious attention to the auditory stimulus being presented to you. If you look closely, you may see that certain details of what you were looking at have faded so that they are either no longer there or they are not there in the same way that they were before. Let us see whether the external form is the same as it was when the discussion began or whether that form has changed somewhat and whether the light and shadows have changed. Is the color as it was before? If you cannot tell, if you really do not know, then the discussion will cease altogether and you can now bring that thing back into visual focus and see how it changed and how much of it was lost. See if it is the same as it was when there was speaking, or whether, when the talking ends, it becomes different. Use your visual sense completely. Try to get back to seeing at least as well as you did before there was talking. You may recognize clearly that the verbal materials presented to you were a thief of your visual perception.

Now, bend your legs again. This time you will be provided with a different kind of auditory distraction. There will be several kinds. Take your legs from side to side and establish your kinesthetic awareness just as completely as you can. Try to make that movement as pleasurable as possible and bring it as fully as possible into your consciousness. (A metronome is started.)

Now, stop moving your legs and just listen. Leave them standing. (Metronome) Listen not only to the metronome but to anything else that you can hear in your environment. (Metronome at slower pace.) Give full awareness to your auditory sense.

Then, take your legs again from side to side while listening. Note if you can discriminate that the metronome no longer is as clear in your consciousness as it was when you were not moving. This should be true of any sound or all sounds that do not absorb the consciousness completely. You would like to hear it as well as before. Stop your movement now and listen again. (Metronome) Notice whether that sound is much more fully available to you than it was when you were moving.

In a moment you will get a nicer sound, a bell. First, the general rule is that one sense, with the average person, will take away some part from another sense. The only exceptions are extremes of pleasure or of pain. Extremes of pain or pleasure will wipe out almost completely all the other sensing. If any other sensation remains, then the pleasure or the pain is to that degree incomplete since pain or pleasure alone can be fullnesses of sensation in themselves. There are other examples that the body is rarely ever exposed to, such as a sound that can so fill consciousness that the body disappears from the awareness and there are no thoughts, nothing but evidently pure awareness of that sound. There are states of consciousness that can be achieved in sensory deprivation chambers, or even better in tanks where the temperature of the water is identical with that of the whole body, where all sensation is lost. However, apart from such rarities, only extremes of pleasure and pain are capable of blotting out other awarenesses.

Now, take your legs again from side to side. Try to give your full awareness to the kinesthetic sense. There will remain a partial awareness of the tactile sense. If your eyes were open, there would be the visual; if there was enough olfactory stimulus, you might partially smell it; and if there is noise, you will have some awareness of that. You should be able to give your awareness very predominantly to the kinesthetic sense. Observe the quality of the awareness that you are giving to the kinesthetic sense. Then, note to what extent it is affected by a sound that is not very loud, not painful, not exceptionally pleasurable, but still a sound that sets up a competition between the kinesthetic and the auditory senses.

First, have a moment of silence and give yourself over to the kinesthetic sense. (Bell) Now continue to move, but give yourself a supremacy of the auditory sense so that you hear just the bell to the extent possible. (Bell) Then, stop moving and just listen. Observe how fully that can occupy your consciousness. (Bell) Then begin moving from side to side slowly, emphasizing auditory awareness. (Bell) Observe whether your experience of the bell is not different. If you doubt it, stop moving altogether for a minute. Once more, just listen. Then stretch out and rest a minute. Scan your body image.

Now, with your eyes open, roll your head from side to side. Try to look at everything that is before your eyes, and see it as clearly as possible. Also, sense as clearly as possible the movement of your head and neck. Try to use your vision and your kinesthetic sense as completely as you can.

Now, at the same time, take your legs from side to side. See everything as clearly as you can and sense your movement as clearly as you can.

Then, forget about your vision for a moment, although you can continue to see clearly if you like or you can close your eyes. However, pay simultaneous attention to the tactile and kinesthetic senses. Feel your body as it rolls over the floor, and notice what you touch, sensations of interaction with the world outside of you, and also the movement. Try to give the greatest possible measure of awareness simultaneously to both. Now, stop moving.

Focus on the tactile. Sense clearly the sensation of touch, and, at the same time, open your eyes and bring in your visual world. Try to touch and see simultaneously as perfectly as possible. Notice whether you can feel that these two senses are functioning in a way that is not so competitive, that you can use them both at one time to an extent that is at least somewhat better than before. Do it without the movement for now.

Then, just be aware of vision. Focus as clearly as you can. Note whether you can maintain that focus while also listening. (Metronome) Try to listen as well as you can and see as well as you can. (Metronome)

Then try, instead, to combine the auditory with the kinesthetic. Listen and move at the same time. Move the legs side to side, or the legs and the head, while also listening. Try to be equally aware of the listening and the movement. (Bell and Metronome)

Now, we will use the bell without shocking you from doing it by surprise. Note if you can integrate your awareness of movement with your auditory awareness and not feel that you are sacrificing one to the other. (Bell) Keenly sense but at the same time listen. (Bell)

Now, we are going to go back to the metronome for a minute. Listen and move, and at the same time be aware of touching. Notice whether you can do those three things without feeling that one dominates or takes away from the others. Observe that you can use your senses in a balanced way. Give a great deal of attention to the pleasurable sensations of movement and to the also pleasurable sensations of touching surfaces as you move. Let the head move. Give attention to the more neutral experience of the metronome. (Metronome) Now stop.

Just continue moving and sensing. We are going to do the bell once more, and you are to use your sense of touch, your sense of movement, your hearing and also your vision. Try to see, hear, touch and sense the movement all at once just as clearly as you can. (Bell) Focus on something visually until it is very clear. Note if you can maintain that focus as you listen. Notice whether you can listen and focus on the movement without losing your vision. Observe whether you can also touch without sacrificing vision or kinesthetic sense or hearing.

Now, find auditory stimuli occurring naturally enough in the room around you and continue to look and to move and to touch in the room or in the environment.

Then, one final time, give yourself completely over to movement. Then, give yourself over completely to touch, or as completely as possible. Give yourself over as completely as possible to listening. (Bell) Give yourself over as completely as possible to vision. Bring everything visual in as clearly as you possibly can—color, form, light, shadow, texture, everything. Then stop.

Now, slowly roll to one side and get up. Move around. Endeavor, as you move, to use all the senses simultaneously and as completely as possible. Pay attention to your movement awareness, to whatever you touch. Be certain that you are using each sense as completely as possible.

If you self-observe closely, you will notice that you can feel a kind of catlike quality about your movements, that they are more primitive. Some people, as they do this exercise, will feel that primitive flavor, especially a catlike quality, to such an extent that they will find that their hands assume a kind of clawlike position. That adds to the experience. The feet pad like the feet of a great cat moving through a jungle.

Again, observe closely, and be sure to tune in each sense. Do not allow yourself to stop seeing as clearly as you can, to stop hearing as clearly as you can. Hear every footfall and sound around you. Sense your own movements, your contact, whatever you touch—whether it be yourself or the environment. Bring them all into the same vital kind of aliveness. Try moving a little more quickly, move as if you were a tiger, a panther, or some very live kind of being whose senses are undiminished by any previous experience. Then come back and sit down a minute.

You should have achieved multisensory awarenesses in varying degrees. It is a difficult exercise in terms of the amount of subtle discrimination that is called for. To some extent, you should feel that you can use the senses together and in a more balanced and integrated way than you ordinarily do, that you can be conscious of all of them simultaneously. Look at your ordinary experience, and you will find that it is a very, very lacking one and that, in fact, as at the beginning of this exercise, one sensation goes a long way towards wiping out the rest, whereas now there is a much more equal and better orchestrated use of them. With practice, this will naturally increase and improve.

Finally, in conclusion, look very closely at any other persons in the room who have done this exercise. Do you notice that people stand out as individuals much more than they ordinarily do? If you look around the room, you will probably see that each of those persons seems somehow better individuated, more potently present. You are likely to find that you are not looking just at a group, but that each person stands forth in his/her own uniqueness, that each one is somehow more clearly defined.

THE HOUSE OF LIFE:
THE FIFTH WAY SCHOOL

A School teaching the Way of the Goddess Sekhmet may be called a House of Life (the ancient Egyptian designation) or, alternatively, a Fifth Way School. Some of the teachings of such a School have been the subject matter of this book.

Psychospiritual exercises of increasing power, and sometimes complexity, normally follow after a thorough practice of the more basic psychophysical exercises such as those found in the books *The Masters Technique* (forthcoming) and *Listening to the Body*, a less comprehensive work. However, the exercises offered here are valuable in and of themselves and will provide self-knowledge which is within the experience of only very, very few. The practice of the exercises, and the results, will become even richer and more rewarding when repeated after having done some of the more basic ones. *Those who are familiar with spiritual disciplines will recognize that, in the case of some of the exercises just presented, the results that are achieved would, by other methods, take weeks or months, or even longer, to obtain.*

All such exercises have the purpose, first of all, of furthering that admonition which is common to all esoteric Schools: KNOW THYSELF! To achieve this, the exercises teach basic mindfulness, concentration and improved use of the self in general—bodily, mentally and emotionally—laying the necessary groundwork for spiritual practices *which will be effective.* In teaching these things,

215

they also *re-educate,* beginning and continuing the sometimes very painful task of *unlearning a great deal of what a person might believe that he/she knows.*

The exercises reproduced here will make easier the always required practices of meditation, the strengthening of the imaging capacities, the acquiring of increasing Presence and Being, and the development of *psychospiritual senses* and the ability to move in a self-regulated way along the continuum of consciousness and into other realities.

The most important practice of all at this stage is the internalizing of the image of the Goddess Sekhmet. When that has been adequately done, then *everything else* will be done more easily, including eventually awakening and integrating the bodies and gaining increasing access to *Sekhmet-as-Teacher!* That is not to say that any of the Work *ever* will become easy. But success will become more possible if the Work of the School otherwise is done well.

As the Work progresses, there will be moments of "waking up" when—and then only—it will be clearly recognized that one has *not been awake before.* Those experiences, in the beginning, will be shocking and painful with respect to the *human condition.* To observe the sleepwalking state of humanity is to understand much about evil and pain and what the saintly Mr. Gurdjieff called "the terror of the situation." But, in the fact that it *is possible* to emerge from that state of sleep there is hope—in fact, the only hope!

The task of exploring the unconscious means, among other things, that the pupil must get to know the many personalities within him/her, what in Fourth Way Work are called the "little I's." Not all of these personalities are either fragmentary or feeble. In fact, what the pupil thinks of ordinarily as him- or herself is usually a constellation of personalities, each seeking dominance. Some are inherited, some acquired, but there is also an essence, a personality that is basically one's own. It must be identified, strengthened and made dominant—or, in some cases, "killed" with a deliberate choice being made to give dominance to one of the others and identify with it.

It has been mentioned that the human being has two souls (although some have one and some have none—a matter that cannot be dealt with here). The BA soul, as the Egyptians knew and practiced, can be "dialogued" with and has its own identity apart from the person without posing any threat to the person's own essential identity, as do the various personalities. The BA, in fact, is sometimes regarded as the "Higher Self"' of a person and can be the source of conscience, morality and ethics, and other important virtues. The BA does not impose these virtues, but can teach the person concerning them and thus be helpful in enabling moral development.

The other soul, the SOKHIM, has the function, in part, of containing as a kind of "blueprint" the personal myth, the entelechy and the essence of the person. These can be learned by achieving a knowledge of the SOKHIM, sometimes with the assistance of the BA, sometimes by exploring the HAIDIT, and sometimes by awakening and integrating with the less subtle bodies that body known as KHU. The awakened and integrated SÂHU has a thorough knowledge of the SOKHIM and an ongoing and intimate relationship and dialogue with the BA.

There are many ways to approach the opening of dialogue with the BA and the knowledge of the SOKHIM. These ways are, of course, important Work in a Fifth Way School or House of Life.

In the Way of the Goddess Sekhmet, some of the most important Work is done with Enneads—Groups of Gods and Goddesses known as The Eight Who, together with the Goddess, constitute a "Ninehood," or an *Ennead*. A pupil may work with one or more of the *Neters* comprising a particular Ennead, as well as with Sekhmet. Some of the most important Work aimed at affecting The War in Heaven is done by magician-priests and -priestesses in the context of the Work of a *Neter* Ennead.

It is also the case that different *Neters* of the Ennead may be Teachers of the various bodies and may help to create a soul, should that be necessary. For each of the bodies there are differing *centers* which need to be successively awakened, differing energy systems, and many different kinds of "foods" for the numerous components of the Five Bodies. One should not expect *ever* to arrive at the completion of such Work.

It must become possible to recognize the conditions of the different bodies of others, and to become able to interact with them. To what extent that can be done will, of course, depend upon one's own condition with respect to one's own bodies. Every existent, even each inanimate object, has at least one subtler level of objective being—something like a KA or Double, although it is not exactly that. But when this is properly understood, then any object, plant, animal, person, and even nonhuman intelligences may be interacted with at the level at which the initiate is able to approach them. Then they may be altered by a mirroring effect which occurs in the body less subtle than the one acted upon—in some cases generating an effect of sequential mirrorings wherein the KHU acts upon the HAIDIT, the HAIDIT upon the KA, and the KA upon the AUFU. It is such effects generated by acting upon the more subtle body that explain most of what is ordinarily termed "magic." It can be used for healing and many other purposes, and there are serious spiritual penalties for misusing this particular knowledge and power. The Teachings of *every* School speak about such possibilities, restrictions and penalties. *The preservation of the pupil's ability to continue to develop* is the main reason for those prohibitions!

These are, of course, but superficial summations of Work which cannot be revealed except to initiates. Although a great deal has been told in this book, the Mysteries and the Hidden Work of the School remain inviolate.

It is intended, however, that much more Fifth Way Work *will be* revealed. While retaining the essential mysteries of the House of Life, it is possible to make known information which can contribute substantially to the elevation of human consciousness in this desperate time when The War In Heaven is intruding ever more fully and terribly upon this earth.

It is that fact, that *intrusion,* which has given rise to the re-entry into human time and space of the Great Mother in these Mysteries manifesting as Sekhmet. To Chaos She comes, bringing terror and a swathe of destruction. By means of Love She comes to re-establish those conditions which alone can preserve the human race and provide for the harmonious development and fulfillment of human beings as individuals, but also as parts of that Great Cosmic Whole *that The War in Heaven is about*—the eventual outcome: *either Being or Nothingness.*

CONCERNING WORK
WITH A FIFTH WAY TEACHER

Those who strongly desire to explore first-hand the very rigorous Fifth Way and Shir-zahd Work should contact the author, providing a full self-description, current photograph and a detailed statement about motivation, expectations and ways in which you think you could contribute to the Work.

Serious requests will be seriously considered. The Way of the Goddess Sekhmet is *not* a Way that can be combined with other philosophies and spiritual disciplines. Total dedication is required, and nothing less is acceptable. The final decision about whether any person is to be accepted into a Fifth Way School is dependent upon the person's being "seized" by the Goddess. An opportunity for such a *HANU* experience will be provided once the individual is considered ready for it. That readiness will be decided by the Teacher or Guide assigned to him or her.

SA SEKHEM SÂHU

GLOSSARY

ANKH: The familiar form of the ankh is a hieroglyphic sign meaning "life" or "live." Objects having the shape of the ankh, of many different sizes and fashioned from various substances, are frequently carried by Gods and Goddesses. The ankh form also is widely used just for ornamental purposes. However, it can be employed as a magic wand when properly prepared for this purpose. The ankh represents both the female and male genitalia and thus is suitable for fertility and (sex) magic. The notion that the sign of the ankh represents a sandal is not to be taken seriously, given its great importance in magic and religion.

APEP: The great Serpent (sometimes called Dragon) who represents the Power of Darkness (Blackness, night) to overcome and swallow up the Light (Day, or that which stands forth from Darkness). It is one function of the Goddess Sekhmet to protect from APEP those Gods who daily must ride across the heavens to prevent the swallowing up of the Light by the Darkness.

AUFU: The gross physical body. The AUFU is a machine, and it differs from "lower animals" only insofar as it is acted upon by the other "higher" and more subtle bodies and the souls.

BA: Often described just as "soul." The BA, although it is not indestructible, is usually "immortal" and reincarnates in one human body after another. The existence of the BA in the body of a woman precedes the impregnation of the ovum. The energy generated by sexual intercourse creates a kind of vortex into which the BA soul is drawn. The BA then draws the sperm to the ovum so that pregnancy typically takes place within a few weeks of the time that the BA entered the woman's body. The BA is a "spirit," material but exceedingly subtle, and it is the individual arena within which is waged The War in Heaven (see separate entry). The BA contains much of both the essence and the entelechy of a person, but other factors will modify these "tendencies" more or less.

BAST: The Sister-Goddess of Sekhmet. She is usually represented as having the head of a cat and the body of a young woman. She is also depicted completely cat-bodied or as a woman with a maneless lion's head. Bast was known to the Egyptians as the Goddess who "catted," giving birth to a litter of children whose fathers were unknown—hence the word "bastard." However, in the older and more correct version of this myth, Bast gave birth without any contact whatsoever with a male so that she is one of the earliest known examples of "immaculate conception." Bast seems to stand in the same relationship to Sekhmet as, for example, the Hawaiian Goddess Pele stands in relation to her Sister-Goddess Kapo.

CACODEMONS: The highest among the evil spirits.

CHAKRAS: (Sanskrit) Energy centers in the gross and subtle bodies. In The Way of the Five Bodies, each of the bodies has its own system of such centers. A High Priest must be able to work with the centers of all of the bodies simultaneously. In the highest form of sexual magic, all of the centers of the Priest and the Priestess must be brought into a connection of sufficient duration and intensity to realize the aim of the Work.

CHAOS: The place of the Powers and Principalities of *Dis*Order. Like Cosmos, Chaos is a realm of such subtlety that it has been mistaken or misunderstood to be Void or Non-Being. Chaos is the Darkness and it is the realm of Evil Gods, Demons, and other Chaotic entities.

COSMOS: The realm of the Powers and Principalities of Order. Cosmos is the "Place" and the "Forces" of Order, Good, Light, Creative Harmony and the Cosmic UrGods. The struggle between Cosmos and Chaos is The War in Heaven.

DEMONIC METAEIDOLONS: Evil Gods, Demons and other Entities serving the Powers and Principalities of Chaos.

DIVINE METAEIDOLONS: Beneficent Gods and Goddesses,

Angels, Demons and other Entities serving the Powers and Principalities of Cosmos.

DRAGONS AND SERPENTS: Among the Names and Epithets of the Goddess Sekhmet are "Ruler of Dragons and of Serpents" and "Great Serpent on the Head of Her Father." Dragon, Serpent and Lion forms are of particular importance in the magical-religious system of the Triad of Memphis and of the Fifth Way. The Dragons and Serpents over which the Goddess Sekhmet rules are those who are Her allies. There are also Dragons and Serpents—foremost among them Apep—who are Her antagonists.

EIGHT GODS OF HERMOPOLIS: One of the Enneads (see below) of Sekhmet.

ENNEAD: An Ennead is a group of nine. In an Ennead of *Neters*, there is one pre-eminent God or Goddess and a group of eight Gods and Goddesses whose energies are worked with by the pre-eminent One. In the case of a group of magicians, one will be the dominant figure who directs the work of the other eight. In a magical Ennead, the magicians (priests and priestesses) may ritually act out the roles of Gods and Goddesses. In such a case, the dominant magician will, of course, act out the role of the pre-eminent God or Goddess. The purpose of the Ennead is to combine the respective energies of the participants so that a new and more powerful current of energy is thereby created. The *direction* of the current created by combining The Eight is provided by the dominant figure. The energy of the dominant figure may also be partially blended with the energy constellation of The Eight—but never to the point of the extinction of consciousness or loss of control by the Leader. In the case of humans ritually enacting the roles of The Eight, individual consciousness may be largely or altogether lost and replaced by that of a Group Spirit, a Being whose identity usually is limited in time by the duration of the collective trance. It is also possible to preserve the existence of this Group Spirit once it has been created. However, it then must be kept subject to restraints.

ESSENTIAL STATUE: In ancient Egypt, statues of the Gods and Goddesses were generally of two kinds—those which were works of art, including monuments, and those which were idols, that is, indwelled by the God or Goddess represented by the sculpture, painting or other image. In the House of Life of the Fifth Way, there were five rooms representing the five bodies of the human being. The first room was very large and was used for physical exercises and other activities requiring a larger space. Anyone attached to the Work of the Goddess Sekhmet was admitted. The room contained a very large statue of the Goddess, Who was present in the statue, but only to the extent required by the simplest and least hidden of the mysteries. As one progressed through the rooms of the Temple, the rooms became smaller, as did the statues. With each increment in size, the statues were progressively more *indwelled* by the Goddess. Only those who had been initiated into the mysteries represented by the particular room (AUFU, KA, HAIDIT, KHU AND SÂHU) were admitted into these rooms.

In the fifth and last room of the Temple, a room into which were admitted only those who had achieved the SÂHU level of self-actualization and initiation, was to be found the smallest statue which was the most completely indwelled by the Goddess. It was always small enough to be easily hidden and transported and was called the *Essential Statue*. The High Priests and High Priestesses would go to any length to prevent such a statue from being stolen or destroyed or from falling into the hands of non-initiates. This statue was believed to contain some part of the Essence of the Goddess and it was the direct Teacher of the High Magician-Priests and -Priestesses.

EUDEMONS: Highest among the good spirits.

FIFTH WAY SCHOOL: This is a House of Life or esoteric School teaching the Way of the Five Bodies of the Goddess Sekhmet. In the Fifth Way School were pupils dedicated completely to the School and the Goddess. There were also pupils who served both the Goddess and the outer worlds of business, politics and other kinds of mundane affairs. As is common with such Schools, the Fifth Way School provided teaching that embraced every area of existence. In the most complete teaching, the pupil progressed through The Way of the Five Bodies to the SÂHU level of self-actualization and initiation and ultimately was given knowledge of the souls of those beings who stand intermediate between humans and the Gods, and finally of the Gods themselves. In some cases, the Goddess Sekhmet imparted to an individual knowledge which is never given to anyone else. As the pupil advanced through The Way, interactions with the Goddess became more frequent and more powerful. To be in such a School was quite literally to "fall into the hands of the Living Goddess." (See also Fourth Way School and Gurdjieff.)

FOURTH WAY SCHOOL: The esoteric School now associated almost exclusively with the Work of G. I. Gurdjieff. The very saintly Mr. Gurdjieff presumably received this Work from the Sufi Order, in particular, the Sarmoun Brotherhood. However, the Gurdjieff Work has very ancient roots in Egypt—a Tradition preserved by the Shir-zahd Order, which is also intimately connected to the Fifth Way Work.

GURDJIEFF: G. I. Gurdjieff brought to the West from Central Asia the teachings often referred to as Fourth Way. It is fairly certain that Mr. Gurdjieff—the most important spiritual figure of the first half of the 20th century—also had links to the Shir-zahd Order and thus to the Fifth Way of the Goddess Sekhmet. Another major figure known to have brought various Shir-zahd (Lion-born) Teachings to the West was the great explorer Sir Richard Francis Burton. Burton's translation of *The Arabian Nights* conceals in both text and footnotes many of the Shir-zahd Teachings. Even the name of the narrator of *The Nights,* Shahrazad (Scheherazade), establishes the link between that Work and the Order. Gurdjieff similarly concealed important Fourth Way Teachings in his magnum opus *All and Everything.*

HAIDIT: This body, also called the Shadow, can be (roughly) identified with what we call "the unconscious," including not only the personal unconscious by parts of the "collective unconscious." The HAIDIT is the third of the five subtle bodies and stands midway between the AUFU and the KA and their worlds on the one hand, and the magical and spiritual bodies and their worlds on the other.

HANU: To be "seized by the God." This "seizing"—usually for some special role or purpose—almost always involved an Idol or Essential Statue (see separate listing) of a God or Goddess. The Deity, indwelling the statue, caused it to move. Most commonly, this movement was a nodding or shaking of the head or a gesture made with the hand and arm. Eye movements and also speech were sometimes reported. The human individual thus "seized by the God" was thereafter temporarily or throughout his/her lifetime—or even for successive incarnations—in the service of that Goddess or God.

HEKAU: Words of power. Consciousness-altering sounds (sometimes gestures, postures and Sacred Movements), ways of activating centers and energy systems of the subtle bodies. HEKAU are used for many other magical and religious purposes, including the capacity to influence even the Cosmos and the Gods.

HOUSE OF LIFE: The ancient Egyptian Mystery School.

IDOL: Any image *indwelled* by a non-human intelligence, or believed to be so. (See Essential Statue.)

IMAGINATION: For the three most subtle bodies—HAIDIT, KHU and SÂHU—the *Creative Imagination* is the "psychosensory system" which gives knowledge of the magico-spiritual realms. In the case of the KA, however, Imagination represents to its consciousness only a reality which largely coincides with the AUFU's. True Creative Imagination is beyond the grasp of the KA, and is approximated by misleading and often dangerous tendencies to engage in *fantasy*.

KA: The double of the AUFU. the KA is *mind,* and its consciousness is of a mental body which mirrors the AUFU to the extent that the KA's awareness is not distorted. When it *is* distorted, then the conscious behavior of the KA will impose those distortions on the AUFU. Loosely speaking, the KA is what we mean by "conscious mind."

KHU: The "magical" and fourth most subtle of the Five Bodies, the KHU ordinarily exists as a latency and becomes conscious (with rare exceptions) only in the case of a person who pursues a magico-spiritual Path which can awaken it. When a man's KHU is awakened and integrated with the three less subtle bodies, then he lives not only in the everyday world of "consensus reality" but also in a supramundane world where he may interact with "spiritual beings," even "Gods."

KUNDALINI: This is the High Creative and Magical Power existing in all of the subtle bodies of the human being. It is usually represented as a coiled serpent which sleeps at the base of the spine until, by appropriate measures, it is awakened and makes its way up to the brain and Crown chakra. Although found in both sexes, the Kundalini energy is female. It is above all a sexual energy, capable of fertilizing the brain and thus effecting transformations and potentiation of consciousness. "Raising Kundalini" can, therefore, be one of the most fulfilling of all possible undertakings. It is also, however, an extremely hazardous undertaking, and madness and death are among the not infrequent outcomes when the effort fails. Kundalini is more often associated with India but was well known in Egypt, especially so within the context of the Goddess Sekhmet. The contemporary magician Kenneth Grant affirms that the Kundalini energy is identical with that of the energy constellation of the Goddess Sekhmet (private communication).

MANTRA: (Sanskrit) HEKAU or Power Words.

MEHENET: The Serpent Goddess who, in the "Myth of the Destruction of Mankind," is an aspect of the Goddess Sekhmet. In that myth and in other contexts as well, Mehenet is the Uraeus serpent on the head of Ra, her father. From this serpent spews forth the energies of the Goddess Nesert, i.e., Flame. In relation to other Gods, Mehenet also takes this (Uraeus) role, as protectress of Osiris, for example.

NEFER-TEM: Son of Sekhmet and Ptah. He is human-bodied and is the God who gave medical knowledge to humans. Nefer-Tem is, therefore, the God of Physicians—later emerging as the Greek God Asclepius, who is still identified with medicine today.

NESERT: A Goddess form of Sekhmet in the "Myth of the Destruction of Mankind." In this context, Nesert is to be understood as the energy constellation of Flame in its destructive aspects. The destruction, however, is used to protect the good and annihilate the wicked. In the aforementioned myth, Nesert as Flame comes forth from the Serpent Goddess Mehenet, who is the Uraeus serpent on the forehead of Ra.

NETER: This term is most often reserved for Gods and Goddesses but can also be properly applied to some other higher and more subtle beings. As the pupil progresses along a spiritual Path, he/she eventually reaches a point beyond which no further progress is possible unless the teacher is a *Neter*. The *Neter* teaches and demonstrates in ways that no human teacher is able to do. Magical and spiritual disciplines done—or attempted to be done—without the guidance of the *Neters* were labeled "Paths of Fools" in most ancient traditions.

PHARAONIC LINE: This refers both to the physical line of genetic inheritance which links successive Pharaohs—a line kept unusually pure by the institution of brother-sister marriage—and also to the body of knowledge restricted to the Pharaohs and handed down directly from one ruler to the next. The Knowledge contained in this Pharaonic Line could only be taught by the Goddess or God (or Goddesses and Gods) who were the Pharaoh's Teacher(s).

PTAH: Creator God and husband-brother of Sekhmet. He created the material world and, at the suggestion of Sekhmet, created the arts. He is also credited with giving to humanity the sciences, mathematics and philosophy. When Ptah is associated with the last-mentioned contributions, then the God Thoth is considered to be the intellect of Ptah.

Although Ptah is the "Creator God," He is pre-existed by Sekhmet, who is considered to be the "Primal and Supreme Creative Power."

SA: The Breath of Life—the animating force by means of which otherwise inanimate matter is enabled to be alive.

SA SEKHEM SÂHU: These are Words of Power (HEKAU) to be chanted as a meditation form or for certain magical purposes. The *mantra* means "The Breath of Life, the Might, the Realized Human."

SÂHU: This is the most subtle of the five subtle bodies and the "highest." The awakening of the SÂHU consciousness can only be achieved by following an effective spiritual Path and by first awakening and integrating each of the less subtle bodies. The SÂHU consciousness contains and integrates AUFU, KA, HAIDIT, and KHU.

SEKHEM: Power or Might. Sekhem is the most formidable of the human potentials and allows its conscious possessor to function both in the human dimension and in the interaction with *Neters*.

SEKTI: "Psychopharmacologist to the Gods." Sekti prepared the intoxicating brew which caused Sekhmet to cease slaughtering humans in the "Myth of the Destruction of Mankind."

SET: Perhaps the oldest Deity known to the human race. Literally, the name means "black." In The Way of the Five Bodies, Set is the great Urgod of Chaos and the principal antagonist of Sekhmet in The War in Heaven. Set is believed to be the prototype of Shaitan or Satan, Lord of Hell. He is thus a personification of the human deep unconscious, of atavisms, but also (partly) of the True Will. (One difficulty with the magic of Aleister Crowley was his failure to recognize that the energy constellation of Set was only *partly* identical with the True Will.)

The oldest Deity known to the human race, along with Set, is the Goddess Sekhmet. Set may precede her in the sense that Nothingness precedes Being, Chaos precedes Order, and Unconsciousness precedes Consciousness. The foregoing is a theoretical construction, and it is not really possible to say which of these Gods preceded the other or whether perhaps they came to be in simultaneity. That they are the oldest Deities—and Beings—is generally accepted in the Egyptian as well as many other spiritual, magical, and occult Traditions.

SEXUAL MAGIC: Procedures utilizing sexual energies for magical purposes.

SEXUAL MYSTICISM: Strictly speaking, sex magical practices which aim at acquiring knowledge of an other—human or non-human—by achieving de-differentiation or oneness with the other.

SHAKTI: (Sanskrit) Power and energy, especially magical power and the power of consciousness to move towards creation and re-creation of self and world. Shakti is of the essence of the energy constellation of the Goddess Sekhmet. Kenneth Grant has pointed out that "The word *Shakti* derives from *Sekh,* which in ancient Egypt denoted heat, particularly sexual heat, exemplified by Sekhmet."

SIDDHIS: (Sanskrit) An Indian term for magical or occult powers.

SOKHIM: This is the "second soul" of a person. Unlike the other soul, the BA, the SOKHIM is mortal and is conceived with and perishes with the individual. The SOKHIM is "born" in the fertilized ovum and will die with the physical body. It is the foundation for consciousness and the link between the body and the mind.

Unlike the BA soul, the SOKHIM did not "dialogue" with the person so that the Egyptian's ignorance concerning it was comparable to our own present-day ignorance concerning our souls, with which we have lost the ability to converse.

SOLAR DISC: A disc representing the sun (Ra) worn on the heads of Gods and Goddesses, and sometimes priests and priest-esses, representing particular *Neters*. The solar disc is usually worn in conjunction with a Uraeus serpent—a standing cobra in front of the disc which stands on or arises out of the head of the Deity.

THOTH: Also known as Tahuti. Thoth is the God of mathe-matics and the sciences and His Book contains the most profound mysteries and Supreme Keys of Magic.

TRIAD OF MEMPHIS: This refers to the great House of Life situated at Memphis where was taught the Ways of the Goddess Sekhmet and the Gods Ptah and Nefer-Tem.

URAEUS: The Uraeus serpent is the standing form of the co-bra, often before the solar disc, which appears on the heads of cer-tain Deities. This serpent may be identified with the Goddess Mehenet who is Herself, in such a case, an aspect of the God or God-dess upon whose head She appears. There are also Goddess forms of the serpent which stand alone, including the Goddess known in In-dia as Kundalini.

URDEMONS: The primal and most powerful amongst good and evil demons.

URGODS: The primal and most powerful amongst the Gods and Goddesses.

URHEK: A very powerful High Magician-Priest or -Priestess, especially one who has a very thorough and effective knowledge of HEKAU (Words of Power).

THE WAR IN HEAVEN: The conflict between Chaos and Cos-mos, the final resolution of which would be the transforming of Chaos into Cosmos or of Cosmos into Chaos. The two realities—Cosmos and Chaos—are primordial, interactive and absolutely an-tagonistic. The War in Heaven exists in all places and throughout time. It is waged within every individual human, and the only "pure" representations of either of these conflicting forces are the great UrGods who confront one another in a struggle.

The Cat Has Let Herself Out of the Bag